The
Mammal Guide
of Southern Africa

Burger Cillié

BRIZA

To Him who created them all

Published by
BRIZA PUBLICATIONS
CK 90/11690/23
PO Box 56569
Arcadia 0007
Pretoria
South Africa
www.briza.co.za

First edition 1997
Second edition, first impression 2004
Second edition, second impression 2007

ISBN 978 1 875093 45 8

Managing editor: Reneé Ferreira
Proofreader: David Pearson
Cover design: Sally Whines, The Departure Lounge
Typesetting: Melinda Stark, Lebone Publishing Services, Cape Town
Reproduction: Hirt & Carter, Cape Town
Castle Graphics, Johannesburg
Printed and bound by Tien Wah Press (Pte) Ltd, Singapore

Photo credits
Cover – Main photograph: African Elephants; top row from left: Cheetah,
Meerkat, White Rhinoceros, Gemsbok, Dwarf Mongoose (Burger Cillié)
Contents – Buck tracks in the sand (Eric Reisinger)
Acknowledgements – Leopard skin (Eric Reisinger)
Introduction – Plains Zebra skin (Eric Reisinger)

CONTENTS

Acknowledgements

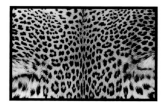

First, I wish to thank in absentia the late Dr Reay Smithers who helped me to compile the book in its original format in 1985. His friendliness, assistance and enthusiasm are still greatly appreciated today. Although he is no longer with us, we are grateful that he was able to leave us his life's work, the "Mammal Bible", *Mammals of the southern African subregion*.

I also wish to express my sincere thanks to all the wildlife photographers, agencies and friends who kindly made their slides available for use in this book.

Thank you to Dr Naas Rautenbach for his help and advice on the new section on small mammals.

A special thanks to Kjeld Kruger of Wambiri Safaris for letting me photograph his collection of droppings.

I also wish to express my gratitude to Briza Publications for the confidence they have displayed in the book by publishing this revised edition. A big thank you to all friends and family members for their ideas, interest and constructive suggestions; and especially to my wife and children for all their help, patience and encouragement.

But most of all, I wish to thank my Creator for the privilege of being able to publish this book in its revised form, in this way sharing again with others a small (animal) part of His wonderful creation.

Burger Cillié

Introduction

This guide is not a textbook for zoologists – although all the facts are zoologically correct. It has been compiled to provide the general public with relevant information about our wild animals. While the emphasis is on identification, the book also contains a great deal of other relevant information about each animal's behaviour, distribution, habitat preference, reproduction, tracks, droppings, etc.

All of the more common mammals that one is likely to come across are discussed and illustrated with the help of good colour photographs. In each case, two photographs (usually of the male and female) have been included and have been selected in such a way that identifying marks are visible. Distinguishing features of animals which may be confused with one another are also highlighted.

The spoor illustration of each animal is of the left back paw. Some animals' front and back paws differ drastically. The front paw illustration is then marked with an "F".

The teeth and horn records were taken from the latest edition of *Rowland Ward's African Records of Big Game*.

The layout has been planned with the emphasis on user-friendliness, and the information has been set out briefly, concisely and logically. Language usage is fairly colloquial so that everybody, even children, will be able to use this book with ease.

The identification key should be helpful in directing beginners to the right group of animals.

The geographical region under discussion is the area south of the Kunene and Zambezi rivers (including the Caprivi).

The following symbols have been used to indicate an animal's conservation status:

EN   Endangered

CR   Critical

VU   Vulnerable

Identification Key

Ungulates

Ungulates include all animals of which the last joint of the toes is covered with a horn-like hoof. This group includes all antelope, pig, zebra and giraffe.

Impalas
Impala are gregarious medium-sized antelope and only males have lyrate horns. They have a distinct reddish-brown colour.
Impala, Black-faced Impala
Pages 16–19

Gazelles
Medium-sized antelope of which males and females have lyrate horns. They have a distinct dark stripe on the sides and are the only gazelles in the Southern African region.
Springbok
Pages 20–21

Antelope with spiral shaped horns
Antelope of which only males have spiral curled horns.
Bushbuck, Nyala, Sitatunga, Greater Kudu
Pages 22–29

Large antelope with horns with a spiral ridge
Large antelope of which males and females have straight horns with a spiral ridge towards the base. Widespread throughout the region.
Eland
Pages 30–31

Large antelope with long straight upward horns
Large antelope of which males and females have long straight upward horns. Associated with the arid parts of this region.
Gemsbok
Pages 32–33

Large antelope with horns curving backwards
Large antelope of which males and females have horns curving backwards.
Sable, Roan
Pages 34–37

Antelope with horns curving forward
Antelope of which only males have horns curving forward.
Waterbuck, Lechwe, Puku, Reedbuck, Mountain Reedbuck
Pages 38–47

Small antelope with short straight horns
Small antelope of which mainly the males have straight, short horns.
Grey Rhebok, Klipspringer, Oribi, Steenbok, Cape Grysbok, Sharpe's Grysbok, Suni, Damara Dik-dik, Grey Duiker, Red Duiker, Blue Duiker
Pages 48–69

Blesboks
Medium-sized dark brown antelope with distinguishing white blaze and belly. Males and females have ridged horns.
Blesbok, Bontebok
Pages 70–73

Hartebeests
Large reddish-brown antelope with elongated faces, backs sloping backwards. Both males and females have horns.
Tsessebe, Red Hartebeest, Lichtenstein's Hartebeest
Pages 74–79

Wildebeests
Dark gregarious cattle-like antelope. Both males and females have horns.
Black Wildebeest, Blue Wildebeest, African Buffalo
Pages 80–85

Zebras
Horse-like animals with black and white stripes.
Plains Zebra, Cape Mountain Zebra, Hartmann's Mountain Zebra
Pages 86–91

Pigs
Stout pig-like animals
Warthog, Bushpig
Pages 92–95

Giraffe
Tall animals with a long neck and legs.
Giraffe
Pages 96–97

Very Large Mammals

Very large browsers with bare greyish skin and large feet.

Elephant
Gigantic animal with a long flexible
trunk and tusks.
African Elephant
Pages 100–101

Rhinos
Very large animals resembling prehistoric
creatures with two horns on the muzzle.
Black Rhinoceros, White Rhinoceros
Pages 102–105

Hippopotamus
Very large barrel-shaped aquatic animal.
Hippopotamus
Pages 106–107

Carnivores

Cat- and dog-like animals that hunt their own prey or are scavengers.

Large cats
Large yellowish cats which hunt their own prey.
Lion, Leopard, Cheetah
Pages 110–115

Smaller cats
Smallish cats, mainly nocturnal, prey
on smaller mammals.
Caracal, Serval, African Wild Cat, Small Spotted Cat
Pages 116–123

Hyaenas
Large dog-like animals with short tails
and backs sloping backwards.
Spotted Hyaena, Brown Hyaena, Aardwolf
Pages 124–129

Dog-like animals
Small dog-like animals with long bushy tails
and large ears.
African Wild Dog, Side-striped Jackal, Black-
backed Jackal, Bat-eared Fox, Cape Fox
Pages 130–139

Mongooses and other small carnivores
Small dog- and cat-like animals with elongated
bodies, short legs and long tails.
Honey Badger, African Civet, Small-spotted Genet,
Large-spotted Genet, Rusty-spotted Genet, Striped
Polecat, Yellow Mongoose, Slender Mongoose,
Kaokoland Slender Mongoose, Large Grey Mongoose
Cape Grey Mongoose, White-tailed Mongoose,
Marsh Mongoose, Banded Mongoose,
Dwarf Mongoose, Meerkat, Spotted-necked Otter,
African Clawless Otter
Pages 140–169

Small Mammals

All the other small browsers, omnivores and insectivores.

Aardvark
A bulky animal with a long snout and long ears.
(Antbear)
Pages 172–173

Pangolin
Armoured reptile-like animal with a
long snout and broad tail.
Ground Pangolin
Pages 174–175

Rock Hyrax
A small stout animal associated with rocky areas.
(Rock Dassie)
Pages 176–177

Canerat
A large greyish rat-like animal
associated with marshes.
Greater Canerat
Pages 178–179

Hedgehog
A very small animal with short black
and white spines.
South African Hedgehog
Pages 180–181

Porcupine
A large rodent with long black and white
spines on the upper parts of the body.
Cape Porcupine
Pages 182–183

Hares/Rabbits
Small animals with long ears and short tails.
Scrub Hare, Cape Hare, red rock rabbits
Pages 184–189

Springhare
A rodent with a kangaroo-like appearance. The conspicuous long tail has a bushy black tip.
Springhare
Pages 190–191

Squirrels
Small rodents with bushy tails.
South African Ground Squirrel, Tree Squirrel
Pages 192–195

Galagos
Small nocturnal animals with furry coats and conspicuous large eyes and ears.
South African Galago, Greater Galago
Pages 196–199

Monkeys
Diurnal animals with long tails and hindlegs, often associated with trees.
Vervet Monkey, Blue Monkey, Baboon
Pages 200–205

Shrews and Elephant Shrews

Small mouse-like animals with long snouts. Elephant shrews have mobile snouts. Their eyes and ears are larger than that of shrews and their hind legs are long and powerful.
Lesser Red Musk Shrew, Eastern Rock Elephant Shrew
Page 206

Golden Moles

Without external eyes, ears and tails. They have long claws on all feet and shovel-like snouts. Subsurface burrowers, their runs showing as elevations.
Hottentot Golden Mole
Page 206

Fruit Bats

Typical dog-like faces with large eyes. The two wing claws distinguish them from insect-eating bats who have only one.
Gambian Epauletted Fruit Bat, Wahlberg's Epauletted Fruit Bat, Egyptian Rousette
Page 207

Insect-eating Bats

Usually large ears and only one wing claw. There are six families: sheath-tailed, free-tailed, vesper, slit-faced, horseshoe and leaf-nosed bats.
Mauritian Tomb Bat, Egyptian Free-tailed Bat, Little Free-tailed Bat, Schreiber's Long-fingered Bat, Banana Bat, Cape Serotine Bat, Egyptian Slit-faced Bat, Geoffroy's Horseshoe Bat, Sundevall's Roundleaf Bat
Page 208–210

Mole Rats

Unrelated to golden moles. They have short legs and powerful teeth. They push mounds of soil up to the surface.
African Molerat
Page 211

Mice and rat-like animals

Includes dormice (nocturnal, squirrel-like animals), dassie rats (rock-living, squirrel-like animals), whistling rats, vlei rats, tree rats, rock mice, gerbils, pouched mice and climbing mice.
Woodland Dormouse, Dassie Rat, Brants' Whistling Rat, Angoni Vleirat, Single-striped Grass Mouse, Four-striped Grass Mouse, Acacia Rat, Namaqua Rock Rat, Bushveld Gerbil, Pouched Mouse, Grey Climbing Mouse
Pages 211–214

Top – Greater Kudu (HPH Photography), Right – Klipspringer (Burger Cillié)

Ungulates

Ungulates include all animals of which the last joint of the toes is covered with a horn-like hoof. This group includes all antelope, pig, zebra and giraffe.

Mass ♂ 47–82 kg.
♀ 32–52 kg.

Length of horns
Average ± 50 cm.
Record 80,96 cm.

Food Leaves and grass.

Life expectancy
± 12 years.

Enemies Spotted hyaena, cheetah, leopard, lion, African wild dog, python.

4,5–5 cm

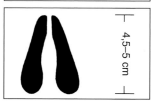

cm 1 2 3 4 5 6 7 8 9

Impala

Rooibok
Aepyceros melampus melampus

Description The colour of the neck, buttocks and back is a shiny reddish-brown. Halfway down the sides the colour grades to light brown and then to grey-white on the belly and chest. The eyes are ringed with white hair and there is a dark spot high on the forehead. The three black stripes, as seen from behind on the buttocks and the tail, are characteristic of this species. The animal has scent glands on the ankles of the hind legs, hidden under a tuft of black hair. The lamb recognises its mother by her scent.

Sexual dimorphism Females lack horns and are smaller than males.

Habitat From open well-wooded areas to fairly dense riverine forest, but usually avoiding mountainous areas. They are dependent on water.

Habits Impala are diurnal, living in herds of approximately 20 animals. In winter the herds join to form larger herds. During the mating season the males establish territories. They gather a group of 15 to 20 females for themselves, chasing other males out of their territory with a roaring snort. Non-territorial males and juvenile males form bachelor herds. Impala are very fast and can jump 3 metres high and 12 metres far. Impala can still be found outside conservation areas.

Voice A warning or alarm sneeze, and in the mating season males make a repeated roaring-snort.

Breeding A single lamb is born from September to January after a gestation period of ± 6½ months.

♂

♀

| Mass | ♂ ± 63 kg. |
| | ♀ ± 50 kg. |

Length of horns
Average ± 46 cm.
Record 67,31 cm.

Food Leaves, grass, shoots, flowers and pods.

Life expectancy
± 12 years.

Enemies Cheetah, leopard, lion, African wild dog, spotted hyaena.

4,5–5 cm

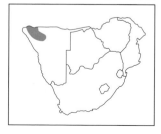

Black-faced Impala

Swartneusrooibok
Aepyceros melampus petersi

Description The colour on the back is dull brown with a blackish-purple sheen. Along the flanks, between the white belly and the dull brown back, is a strip of light brown hair. On the face is a black blaze, and on the tail and the back of the buttocks there are vertical black stripes. The cheeks and ears are reddish-brown. The Black-faced Impala differs from the Impala on account of the black blaze on the face, the longer shaggier tail and the darker coloured upper parts which lack the red sheen of the Impala's coat.

Sexual dimorphism Only males have horns and they are larger than females.

Habitat Dense riverine undergrowth surrounded by open woodland.

Habits Black-faced Impala are diurnal animals which form small herds of 3 to 20, consisting of a male with females and young ones. Other males remain solitary or form male herds. During the lambing season large gatherings take place, which later break up into smaller herds. At night herds sleep together in open areas. They feed during the cooler part of the day and rest in thickets when it is hot.

Voice An alarm sneeze which is sometimes repeated.

Breeding A single lamb is born from December to January after a gestation period of ± 6½ months.

♂

♀

Mass	♂ 33–48 kg.
	♀ 30–44 kg.

Length of horns
Average ± 35 cm.
Record 49,21 cm.

Food Grass, leaves, shoots of karoo bush and herbs.

Life expectancy
± 10 years.

Enemies Brown hyaena, spotted hyaena, cheetah, leopard, lion, African wild dog.

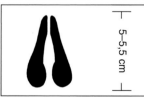

5–5,5 cm

cm 1 2 3 4 5 6 7 8

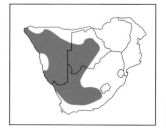

Springbok

Springbok
Antidorcas marsupialis

Description This is South Africa's national animal. The colour is a very light brown with darker brown stripes along the flanks which separate the light brown of the body from the white of the belly. On the back there is a ridge of long, white hair with stripes of brown hair on either side, which is erected when the animal is alarmed or when it runs with a characteristic bouncing motion. The face is white with brown stripes from the eyes to the corners of the mouth. Chocolate-brown or predominantly white animals are sometimes found in the same herd with other animals.

Sexual dimorphism Females have a slighter build than males.

Habitat Open, dry shrubby veld, grass plains or dry riverbeds.

Habits Springbok are gregarious animals which form small herds and congregate into huge herds during spring. Mixed herds, bachelor herds and solitary territorial males are also found. They graze early in the morning and late in the afternoon but rest during the heat of day. Seeing them run is a remarkable experience: the head is kept low and the hair on the back bristles. They hop with their legs held rigidly and in this way they are able to jump high and move forward rapidly over the veld.

Voice A low-pitched growl-bellow, or a high-pitched whistling snort for an alarm call.

Breeding A single lamb is born any time of the year after a gestation period of ± 6 months, peaking in the rainy season.

♂

Burger Cillié

♀

Ulrich Oberprieler

Mass ♂ 40–77 kg.
♀ 30–36 kg.

Length of horns
Average ± 26 cm.
Record 51,44 cm.

Food Mainly leaves,

and flowers.

Life expectancy
± 11 years.

Enemies Leopard, lion,
caracal, python.

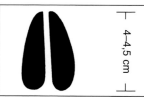

4–4,5 cm

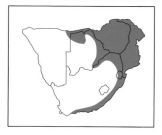

Bushbuck

Bosbok
Tragelaphus scriptus

Description The colouring of the male varies from brown to dark brown and that of the female from light brown to chestnut. Both sexes have white spots on the legs, a white patch on the throat and a white band at the base of the neck. There are white spots on the buttocks and the tip of the tail is also white. Some animals have vertical white stripes on the flanks, which are characteristic of the reddish-brown Chobe Bushbuck, which has more white spots on the flanks. The female differs from the Nyala female by being smaller and having fewer or even no vertical stripes.

Sexual dimorphism Females are smaller, lack horns and are lighter in colour than males.

Habitat Thickets or riverine bush near water.

Habits Bushbuck are shy, solitary antelopes but pairs or small groups of females and young animals are found. The males are very courageous and will attack and sometimes kill leopards, dogs and even human beings. During the day they rest in thickets, coming out late in the afternoon and grazing until late at night. Home ranges are smaller in winter than in summer. All their senses are well developed, which is probably why they still survive outside conservation areas.

Voice A loud bark like that of a baboon.

Breeding A single lamb is born any time of the year after a gestation period of ± 6 months.

♀

♂

♂

Burger Cillié

Chobe

Daryl Balfour/Gallo

| Mass | ♂ 92–126 kg. |
| | ♀ 55–68 kg. |

Length of horns
Average ± 60 cm.
Record 83,19 cm.

Food Mainly leaves but also freshly sprouting grasses, fruit, flowers and pods.

Life expectancy
± 13 years.

Enemies Spotted hyaena, leopard, lion.

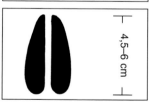

4,5–6 cm

Nyala

Njala
Tragelaphus angasii

Description The Nyala has a slender build and moves gracefully. The male is dark blue-grey in colour with white vertical stripes, yellow-stockinged legs and a white chevron mark between the eyes. The mane on the neck and back is white tipped. Old males have a long fringe of hair under the belly and at the back of the buttocks. The female is reddish-brown to chestnut, with similar stripes and marks but without the chevron between the eyes. The Nyala female differs from the Bushbuck female in that it has more vertical stripes and is larger in size.

Sexual dimorphism Only males have horns. They are also darker in colour and larger than females.

Habitat Thickets and dense bush along rivers in dry woodland. They are dependent on water.

Habits Nyala live in small, loosely knit herds of 3 to 16 animals. Temporary young male herds and female herds are also found. The herd consists of one male, females and young. Members move freely among groups. Old males are solitary or form small herds. They browse by day and by night, especially in the late afternoon, and rest during the heat of day. They are fond of browsing under trees where baboons and monkeys have dislodged fruit.

Voice A bleat and a deep bellow-bark.

Breeding A single calf is born any time of the year after a gestation period of ± 7 months, peaking in August to December and May.

♂

♀

Burger Cillié

Ulrich Oberprieler

Mass ♂ ± 114 kg.
♀ ± 55 kg.

Length of horns
Average ± 60 cm.
Record 82,55 cm.

Food The umbels of papyrus, young reeds and aquatic grasses.

Life expectancy
± 19 years.

Enemies Lion, crocodile.

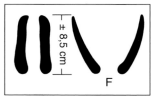

± 8,5 cm

F

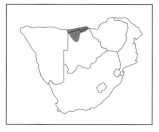

Sitatunga

Sitatunga
Tragelaphus spekei

Description A shy antelope with long hair and a white chevron mark between the eyes. The male is dark grey-brown while the female is usually lighter, yellowish to reddish-brown, with distinct white spots on the flanks and buttocks. The vertical white stripes on the flanks are usually absent or very faint in the southern African species. There is a white patch on the throat and a white band at the base of the neck. The hooves are very long and splayed to ensure a good, firm footing on wet muddy ground. Sitatungas are larger than Bushbucks and have longer horns.

Sexual dimorphism Females are much smaller, lack horns and are usually lighter in colour than males.

Habitat The permanent flooded areas (with papyrus and common reeds) of the Okavango Delta and Linyanti River.

Habits Sitatungas are usually solitary or occur in pairs, but are always connected to a small, loosely knit herd of up to six animals consisting of a male, a few females and juveniles. They can swim well and if disturbed, take to the water. During the day they feed in the reed and papyrus beds in the swamp, avoiding open floodplains. During the heat of day they rest on platforms formed from dry reeds and other vegetation. At night they sometimes move to surrounding dry woodland and return to the swamps again before daylight.

Voice A repeated alarm bark, more drawn-out than that of the bushbuck.

Breeding A single calf is born any time of the year, peaking in June to July.

♂ Phillipe Dejace/Wildfile Pictures

♀ Daryl Balfour

Mass	♂ 190–270 kg.
	♀ 120–210 kg.

Length of horns
Average ± 120 cm.
Record 187,64 cm.

Food Leaves, growth tips of plants, pods and sometimes fresh green grass.

Life expectancy
± 14 years.

Enemies Spotted hyaena, cheetah, leopard, lion, African wild dog.

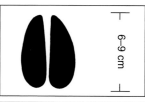

6–9 cm

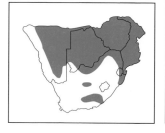

Greater Kudu

Koedoe
Tragelaphus strepsiceros

Description A large antelope with a stately bearing. The colour is pale grey to brownish-grey with a number of vertical white stripes on the flanks. The male's neck becomes darker with age. Between the eyes there is a white chevron marking. Females look similar to the males but without the horns their ears are very prominent, being large and rounded, with a white fringe. The tail is white underneath and there is a conspicuous hump on the shoulders.

Sexual dimorphism Females are smaller than males and lack horns.

Habitat Savannah with enough trees or scrub, especially close to koppies, mountains or along creeks, and close to water.

Habits These diurnal animals browse in the early morning and in the late afternoon. They form family groups of 5 to 12 animals, consisting mostly of females and calves, except in the mating season. Males form separate herds or become solitary. They are graceful and athletic and can jump very high (± 2 m) for such large animals. When the males move fast through trees they keep their heads tilted backwards with their horns held close to their backs. Greater Kudu are still fairly common outside conservation areas.

Voice A very loud bark.

Breeding A single calf is born from November to January after a gestation period of ± 7 months.

Also known as Kudu.

♂

HPH Photography

♀

Burger Cillié

Mass	♂ ± 700 kg.
	♀ ± 460 kg.

Length of horns
Average ± 60 cm.
Record 114,3 cm.

Food Leaves and grass in spring. They drink water regularly when available.

Life expectancy
± 12 years.

Enemy Lion.

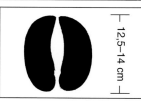

12,5–14 cm

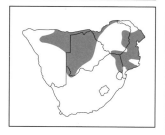

Eland

Eland
Tragelaphus oryx

Description The Eland is the region's largest antelope. The colour is greyish-brown, the male developing a bluish-grey neck as it grows older. The northern species (Livingstone's Eland) has faint vertical white stripes down the flanks. A grown male reminds one of a Brahman bull because of the hump and dewlap. Both sexes have straight horns with a slightly curved edge, a tassel of long brown hair on the forehead, and dark brown hair along the top of the back.

Sexual dimorphism Males are larger than females, with shorter and stouter horns.

Habitat Widely spread in shrubby flat veld, all types of woodland to humid, mountainous grasslands.

Habits Eland usually form small herds of 8 to 12 animals, but very large herds are not uncommon. They usually graze during the day, but in the rainy season they will sometimes graze well into the night, ranging widely in search of food. Eland are nervous animals, taking flight at the slightest sign of danger. They are surprisingly good jumpers, considering their bulk, clearing a height of 2 metres with ease. Serious fights between males sometimes occur. A typical "click" sound is heard as they walk.

Voice Females "moo", calves bleat and males bellow. They sometimes also make a barking sound.

Breeding A single calf is born any time of the year after a gestation period of ± 9 months, peaking in August to October.

Burger Cillié

♂

♀

Koos Delport

| Mass | ♂ ± 240 kg. |
| | ♀ ± 210 kg. |

Length of horns
Average ± 85 cm.
Record 125,10 cm.

Food Grass. Also succulent tubers, tsamma melons and other fruit.

Life expectancy
± 19 years.

Enemies Spotted hyaena, lion, African wild dog.

10,3–11,5 cm

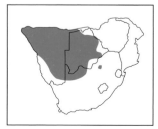

Gemsbok

Gemsbok
Oryx gazella

Description The colour varies from light brown to ash grey with lighter patches on the buttocks. The tail is black with long hair. The animal has a dark brown stripe low down on the flanks which joins up with the dark brown on the upper legs. The rest of the legs and the belly are white. On the crop is a patch of brown which joins up with the brown colouring of the top of the back. The face is white with a black patch on the snout. A smaller black patch high on the forehead, and two black stripes beginning around the eyes, extend down the sides of the face and join the black stripe on the throat. Both sexes have the characteristic long, straight horns.

Sexual dimorphism Females have a lighter build than males and their horns are longer and thinner.

Habitat Open grass plains in semi-desert regions and dry savannah.

Habits Gemsbok live in herds of 12 or more animals. Adult males are territorial and are solitary, or form small herds of 2 to 3. Other herds consist of females, juveniles and calves. After birth, calves are hidden for a few months before they are brought into the herd by their mothers. Gemsbok often kneel while grazing and can survive for long periods without water.

Voice A cattle-like bellow.

Breeding A single calf is born any time of the year after a gestation period of ± 9 months.

♂

♀

Mass	♂ 230–300 kg.
	♀ 220–250 kg.

Length of horns
Average ♂ ± 75 cm.
Record 99,06 cm.

Food Only certain types of grass (up to 8 cm), but also leaves and fruit.

Life expectancy
± 19 years.

Enemies Leopard, lion, crocodile.

10,5–11 cm

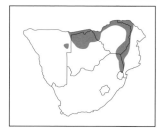

Roan Antelope

Bastergemsbok
Hippotragus equinus

Description This animal is pale reddish-brown in colour and has a darker, erect mane. The legs are slightly darker than the upper parts while the belly is lighter, the tail being dark brown to black. The face is black and mask-like, emphasising the white patches in front of the eyes and around the mouth. Roans have conspicuously long ears. Both males and females have horns, curving backwards like those of the Sable Antelope, but they are shorter in length.

Sexual dimorphism Females are slightly smaller than males and the horns are thinner.

Habitat Open woodland near water with large areas of medium to tall grass. They avoid areas with short grass or thickets.

Habits Roan are diurnal animals forming breeding herds of 5 to 25 animals, with a dominant female as leader as well as a dominant male. The breeding herds are confined to their territories. The dominant male will defend its females from other males. Young males form small groups, while other adult males are solitary. These animals graze in the early morning and late afternoon, resting during the heat of day. Males are often involved in fights, while both sexes defend themselves ably against predators.

Voice A blowing snort.

Breeding A single calf is born any time of the year after a gestation period of 9 to 9½ months.

Also known as Roan.

♂

♀

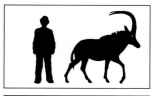

Mass ♂ 200–270 kg.
♀ 180–250 kg.

Length of horns
Average ♂ ± 102 cm.
Record 154,31 cm.

Food Mainly grass, but they browse occasionally. They drink water regularly.

Life expectancy
± 17 years.

Enemies Leopard, lion, crocodile.

8–10,2 cm

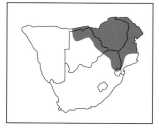

Sable Antelope

Swartwitpens
Hippotragus niger

Description Both males and females have scimitar-like horns which curve backwards. The colouring is dark brown but becomes darker with age. The belly and the back of the buttocks underneath the tail are white. The female is dark brown in colour whereas the calf is a light brown. The face is white with three black stripes, one of which originates between the eyes and extends to the nose; the other two stripes begin around the eyes and extend down the sides of the face to the mouth. The calf looks very similar to the Roan Antelope's calf, but as it remains close to its parents it cannot be mistaken for a Roan.

Sexual dimorphism Females are slightly smaller, and usually more brown in colour than males. Their horns are also shorter.

Habitat Open woodland with medium to long grass on well-drained soil. They are always close to water and avoid thickets and areas with short grass.

Habits They form herds of between 10 and 40 animals, a herd usually consisting of some females with their calves and juveniles. Young males form small herds, while older males are territorial and solitary. Sable Antelopes are diurnal and normally graze in the early morning or late afternoon, resting during the hottest part of the day. They are able to defend themselves well against predators, even lions. They will back up against a bush and await their attackers with their heads lowered, using their powerful horns to great effect.

Voice Snorting, sneezing and bellowing.

Breeding A single calf is born from January to March after a gestation period of ± 8 months.

Also known as Sable.

♂

Burger Cillié

♀

Burger Cillié

| Mass | ♂ 250–270 kg. |
| | ♀ 205–250 kg. |

Length of horns
Average ± 75 cm.
Record 99,70 cm.

Food Grass, sometimes leaves and fruit. They drink water regularly.

Life expectancy
± 14 years.

Enemies Spotted hyaena, lion, cheetah, African wild dog.

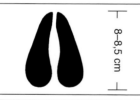

8–8,5 cm

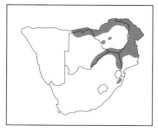

Waterbuck

Waterbok
Kobus ellipsiprymnus

Description A big antelope with a characteristic white circle around the tail and a collar of white hair around the neck and the snout. The rest of the body is grey-brown. There are white stripes on the ridges of the eyebrows and the chin is white. The tuft on the end of the tail as well as the lower legs are darker and more brown in colour. The hair is shaggy, coarse and long.

Sexual dimorphism Males are larger than females, which are hornless.

Habitat Areas near rivers or marshes and dry floodplains. They are never far from water.

Habits Waterbuck are diurnal, gregarious animals. The small herds of 6 to 12 animals consist mostly of females, calves and young. Males are territorial and while some remain solitary, others form male herds. Serious fights between male Waterbuck are more common than similar fights among other species of antelope. When danger threatens they take to the water, even if there are crocodiles about. Crocodiles do not usually attack Waterbuck, probably on account of the unpleasant smell given off by their skin.

Voice Not often heard. Snoring sound when alarmed or excited. Females call calves with a soft "muh".

Breeding 1, seldom 2, calves are born any time of the year after a gestation period of ± 9 months.

♂

♀

Mass ♂ 100–130 kg.
  ♀ 61–97 kg.

Length of horns
Average ± 70 cm.
Record 88,90 cm.

Food Watergrass and other grass on the fringes of vleis. They drink water regularly.

Life expectancy
Unknown.

Enemies Cheetah, lion.

6,5–7,5 cm

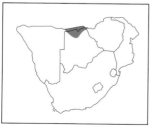

Lechwe

Rooilechwe
Kobus leche

Description A medium-sized antelope with the shoulders lower than the crop, causing the body to slope forward. The colouring is a bright reddish-brown, lighter lower down the body and becoming white on the belly. The throat and insides of the legs are white and there are characteristic black stripes on the front legs. The hooves are somewhat splayed and longer than those of other antelope, ensuring a better footing in marshy areas. Pukus are smaller than the Lechwe, more golden brown, with less white on the bellies and lacking the black markings on the front legs.

Sexual dimorphism Females are smaller than males and lack horns.

Habitat Limited to shallow flooded marshes and vleis and along large rivers, and floodplains along large rivers.

Habits Lechwe form herds ranging from 10 to approximately 30 animals. The herds consist of females and young, or males. Some males establish territories during the mating season and will chase away other males. When danger threatens these animals take to the water. They cannot move fast on dry land and run with their heads held characteristically low. They are fond of grazing in the early mornings or late afternoons in shallow water on the floodplains. During the daytime they rest on dry islands in the swamp, and at night they sleep near the waterside.

Voice Whinnying-grunt as a warning call and a low-pitched whistling sound.

Breeding A single lamb is born any time of the year after a gestation period of 7 to 8 months, peaking in October to December.

♂

♀

Mass ♂ 68–91 kg.
♀ 48–80 kg.

Length of horns
Average ± 45 cm.
Record 56,20 cm.

Food Grass, but sometimes browse on thorn trees. They drink water regularly.

Life expectancy
Unknown.

Enemies Cheetah, leopard, lion, African wild dog.

± 6 cm

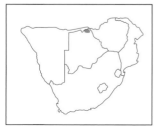

Puku

Poekoe
Kobus vardonii

Description A well-built, medium-sized antelope with a straight back. The colouring is a golden brown over most of the body, becoming slightly lighter under the belly and darker on the forehead. A small area above the eyes and around the mouth is white and the ears have black margins. The Puku can be distinguished from the Lechwe by its smaller size and by the absence of the black stripes on the front legs.

Sexual dimorphism Females are smaller than males and lack horns.

Habitat The grassy plains between floodplains and the surrounding woodlands.

Habits Puku form herds of 6 to 28 animals consisting of females and young. Adult males are territorial and are solitary, while other males form bachelor herds. Members move freely among herds. During the mating season the territorial male rounds up a number of females passing through its territory. One of its major occupations is then to keep the females together. These animals usually graze early in the morning and in the late afternoon, even until after dark.

Voice A repeated alarm whistle.

Breeding A single lamb is born any time of the year after a gestation period of ± 8 months, peaking in May to September.

♂

♀

| Mass | ♂ ± 80 kg. |
| | ♀ ± 70 kg. |

Length of horns
Average ± 30 cm.
Record 46,67 cm.

Food Grass. They drink
water regularly.

Life expectancy
± 9 years.

Enemies Spotted hyaena,
cheetah, leopard, lion,
African wild dog, python.

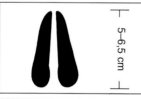

Reedbuck

Rietbok
Redunca arundinum

Description The body is a yellowish grey-brown, the throat and chest grey-white and the belly white. The forelegs are dark brown in front and there are often small, black, glandular areas below the ears. The tail is bushy, with white underneath. The Reedbuck could be confused with the Impala and the Mountain Reedbuck, but lacks the three black stripes seen on the hindquarters of the Impala. The Impala is also redder than the Reedbuck. The Mountain Reedbuck is smaller and more greyish and its habitat differs.

Sexual dimorphism Only males have horns, and they are larger than females.

Habitat Vleis, reedbeds and dry floodplains close to water.

Habits Reedbuck are not gregarious and usually appear in pairs occupying a territory, while larger groups are also seen temporarily during the winter months. They are always near water. During the heat of day they rest in reedbeds or long grass, grazing during the cooler parts of the day and even at night. They run with a typical rocking-horse movement with the tail held high, displaying the white underneath.

Voice A high-pitched alarm whistle.

Breeding A single lamb is born any time of the year after a gestation period of 7½ to 8 months.

Also known as Southern Reedbuck.

♂

Burger Cillié

♀

Burger Cillié

| Mass | ♂ 24–36 kg. |
| | ♀ 15–34 kg. |

Length of horns
Average ± 14 cm.
Record 29,21 cm.

Food Mainly grass. They drink water regularly.

Life expectancy
± 11 years.

Enemies Leopard, python, brown hyaena.

± 4,5 cm

Mountain Reedbuck

Rooiribbok
Redunca fulvorufula

Description A medium-sized antelope with a long, hairy coat. The colour is grey with a reddish sheen and the neck is brown. The belly is white, the tail bushy with white underneath and there are black spots below the ears. The horns curve forward at about the level of the tips of the ears. The ears are rounded with a white fringe. The Mountain Reedbuck differs from the Grey Rhebok which is more grey-brown, has a longer, thinner neck and more pointed and erect ears.

Sexual dimorphism Males are slightly larger than females, which are hornless.

Habitat Rocky slopes of mountains, hills and koppies with sufficient food and shelter.

Habits Mountain Reedbuck are gregarious, living in herds of 3 to 6 animals, but bigger herds have also been observed. Males are territorial and solitary or form bachelor herds, while other herds consist of females and juveniles. These animals are wary but inquisitive. During the heat of day they usually rest in the shade. They graze and drink water early in the morning, the late afternoon or even at night. They run with a typical rocking-horse movement, the white underparts of the tail showing.

Voice A sharp alarm whistle.

Breeding A single lamb is born any time of the year after a gestation period of ± 8 months, peaking in December to January.

♂

Burger Cillié

♀

HPH Photography/Photo Access

| Mass | ♂ 18–23 kg. |
| | ♀ 18–21 kg. |

Length of horns
Average ± 20 cm.
Record 30,16 cm.

Food Exclusively grass.

Life expectancy
± 9 years.

Enemies Cheetah,
leopard.

± 4 cm

Grey Rhebok

Vaalribbok
Pelea capreolus

Description This animal is of medium build, grey-brown in colour, and its hair is thick and woolly. The belly and the underparts of the tail are white. The neck is long and thin, and the ears are long, erect and pointed, which distinguishes it from the Mountain Reedbuck. The horns are straight and erect and conform with the ears. The Grey Rhebok lacks the black spots below the ears which are characteristic of the Mountain Reedbuck. The horns of the latter also curve slightly forward.

Sexual dimorphism Females lack horns and have a lighter build than males.

Habitat Open mountain slopes or plateaus with grass plains. They are not dependent on water.

Habits Grey Rhebok are gregarious and form family groups of up to 12 animals which consist of a male, females and young animals. There are no male herds. Other males are territorial and solitary. These animals graze at any time of the day, taking short rests, but they always rest during the heat of day. They are very alert and flee when there is danger. They run with a rocking motion, the white underparts of the tail showing.

Voice Snort and an alarm cough.

Breeding A single lamb is born from December to January after a gestation period of ± 8½ months.

♂

Burger Cillié

♀

Burger Cillié

| **Mass** ♂ 9–12 kg. |
| ♀ 11–16 kg. |

| **Length of horns** |
| **Average** ± 8 cm. |
| **Record** 16,19 cm. |

Food Mainly leaves, but sometimes grass.

Life expectancy ± 7 years.

Enemies Leopard, lion, caracal, python.

± 2 cm

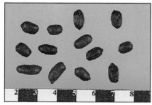

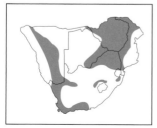

Klipspringer

Klipspringer
Oreotragus oreotragus

Description A small antelope with a thick, spiny coat providing protection against injury when it bumps against rocks. The colouring varies from yellow to grey-brown to dull grey with fine black speckles, providing good camouflage among the rocks. The short tail is the same colour as the body while the belly is white. In front of the eyes are large black, tear-shaped markings. The horns are short, erect and curved slightly forward at the tips. Klipspringers are stouter than duikers, which also lack the tear marks.

Sexual dimorphism Females lack horns and are larger than males.

Habitat On or near rocky hills, koppies or mountains. They are not dependent on water.

Habits Klipspringers are solitary, found in pairs or family groups. Males establish territories which they scent-mark. These animals are often seen standing motionless on high rocks. They are very nimble, jumping and moving very quickly up steep rock faces. (They move on the tips of their hooves.) They rest in the shade during the heat of day and graze early in the morning or late in the afternoon.

Voice A very loud, high-pitched forced expiration of air as an alarm call.

Breeding A single young is born any time of the year after a gestation period of 7 to 7½ months.

Burger Cillié

♂

Niel Cillié

♀

| Mass | ♂ 11–17 kg. |
| | ♀ 8–20 kg. |

Length of horns
Average ± 10 cm.
Record 19,05 cm.

Food Grass. They do not drink water.

Life expectancy
± 13 years.

Enemies Cheetah, leopard, lion, caracal, African wild dog.

± 4 cm

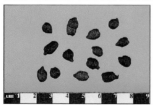

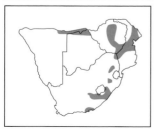

Oribi

Oorbietjie
Ourebia ourebi

Description A small antelope with a light rusty-brown colouring, white throat and belly. The horns are straight but are curved slightly forward towards the tips. White spots occur alongside the nostrils and above the eyes. The tail is black on top and white underneath, and black spots are present below the ears. The Oribi is distinguished from the Steenbok by its larger size and by the black tail. The white area on the belly is also larger and the neck is thinner and longer.

Sexual dimorphism Females lack horns and are usually slightly larger than males.

Habitat Open grass plains or floodplains with sufficient water.

Habits Oribi are solitary animals but sometimes form family groups or temporary herds of up to 12 animals. Males are territorial and maintain their territories for the mating season. During the heat of day the animals rest in the grass. They prefer to graze when it is cooler. When alarmed they leap up and run away in a bouncing fashion. They are inquisitive and after a certain distance will turn around and look back, and may even walk back. They use communal manure heaps.

Voice A snorting alarm whistle.

Breeding A single lamb is born from October to December after a gestation period of ± 7 months.

♂

Burger Cillié

♀

Burger Cillié

| Mass | ♂ 9–13 kg.
♀ 11–13 kg. |

Length of horns
Average ± 9 cm.
Record 19,05 cm.

Food Grass and leaves but also roots and bulbs. They very seldom drink water.

Life expectancy
± 6 years.

Enemies Cheetah, leopard, lion, caracal, African wild dog, martial eagle, python.

3–4 cm

Steenbok

Steenbok
Raphicerus campestris

Description The colour varies from light brown to a darker brick-brown. The belly, the insides of the legs and the underside of the tail are white. The horns are erect, straight and very sharp. The Steenbok is a small antelope which still occurs reasonably abundantly. It can be distinguished from the Oribi by the absence of both the black on top of the tail and the black spot below the ears. It also has a smaller build and a shorter neck than the Oribi. The Grysbok has characteristic white speckles on the body.

Sexual dimorphism Males have horns and have a slighter build than females.

Habitat Open grassveld (not short grass), avoiding craggy or mountainous terrain. They are not dependent on water.

Habits Steenbok are found singly or in pairs. During the heat of day they lie down in the shade. They graze when it is cooler, and even at night. They establish territories with manure heaps on strategic points, scent-marked by males and females with their glands. When alarmed they often lie down on the ground but jump up at the last moment, relying on their quick-footed ability, to escape.

Voice A soft bleat.

Breeding 1, occasionally 2, lambs are born any time of the year after a gestation period of ± 6 months, peaking in November to December.

♂

♀

Mass 9–12 kg.

Length of horns
Average ± 8 cm.
Record 13,34 cm.

Food Grass and leaves but also fruit. They can go without water for long periods.

Life expectancy
Unknown.

Enemies Leopard, caracal.

3–3,5 cm

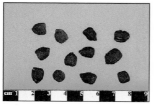

Cape Grysbok

Kaapse Grysbok
Raphicerus melanotis

Description The colour is dark reddish-brown with white speckles. The throat, belly and insides of the legs are a lighter yellow-brown. This small antelope has long, pointed ears with short, erect horns. It is slightly smaller and darker in colour than Sharpe's Grysbok. It differs from the Steenbok in that it has white speckles on the body and prefers a more dense habitat.

Sexual dimorphism Only the males have horns.

Habitat Bushy undergrowth along rivers and at the foothills of mountains. They are not dependent on water.

Habits Cape Grysbok are solitary animals, except during the mating season when they are found in pairs. They usually move slowly and carefully with their heads held low. They lie flat on the ground when danger threatens, waiting until the last moment before fleeing. They are mainly nocturnal but also graze in the late afternoon. During the heat of day they rest under thick shelter.

Voice Bleating screams when caught, otherwise quiet.

Breeding A single lamb is born from September to October after a gestation period of ± 6 months.

Also known as Grysbok.

♂

Burger Cillié

Ulrich Oberprieler

♀

Mass ♂ ± 8 kg.	
♀ ± 7,5 kg.	

Length of horns
Average ± 6 cm.
Record 10,48 cm.

Food Leaves, shoots, roots, fruit and young grass sprouts.

Life expectancy
Unknown.

Enemies Leopard, lion, caracal, python.

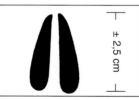

± 2,5 cm

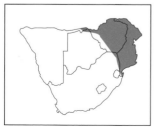

Sharpe's Grysbok

Tropiese Grysbok
Raphicerus sharpei

Description The colour is light brown around the neck and reddish-brown with white speckles on the body. The belly and insides of the legs are white, the horns are very short and erect, and the large ears have rounded tips. This small antelope differs from the Cape Grysbok by being lighter in colour and having more rounded ears and a more pointed face. Its white speckles and preference for a denser habitat distinguishes it from the Steenbok.

Sexual dimorphism Females are slightly larger than males and lack horns.

Habitat Areas with low to medium grass and scrub in woodland. They are not dependent on water.

Habits Sharpe's Grysbok are solitary animals except during the mating season when they may be seen in pairs. They are mainly nocturnal but also browse during cool, cloudy mornings or late afternoons. During the heat of day they rest under thick shelter. When alarmed they run away with their heads held low, almost in a crouching position - this distinguishes them from other small antelope.

Voice Bleating screams when caught, otherwise quiet.

Breeding A single lamb is born any time of the year after a gestation period of ± 7 months.

♂

Burger Cillié

♀

Burger Cillié

Mass	♂ 4,5–5,2 kg.
	♀ 5,1–6,8 kg.

Length of horns
Average ± 8 cm.
Record 13,34 cm.

Food Leaves and fruit.
They do not drink water.

Life expectancy
Unknown.

Enemies Leopard, python.

± 2 cm

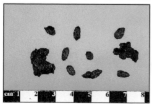

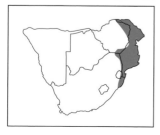

Suni

Soenie
Neotragus moschatus

Description The colour of this very small antelope varies from dull light brown to light reddish-brown with lighter speckles on the upper parts. The belly, insides of the legs and throat are white. The tail is long and dark with a white margin and is white underneath. The upper lip is longer than the lower lip, and the horns are straight and slope backwards in line with the face. The Suni can be distinguished from the Steenbok and Duiker by its smaller build, smaller ears, the backward-sloping horns and the length and colouring of the tail.

Sexual dimorphism Only the males have horns and have a lighter build than females.

Habitat Thickets in dry woodland. They are not dependent on water.

Habits As Suni are very shy, they are seldom seen. They are usually solitary but are also found in pairs or family groups. During the hottest part of the day they rest in thick shelter, and browse in the early morning and late afternoon. When alarmed they usually stand motionless for quite some time before running away. They move silently and the continuous swinging of their tails is often the only movement which betrays their presence. They use communal manure heaps.

Voice Snorting and a high "chee-chee" whistle as they run away.

Breeding A single lamb is born from August to February after a gestation period of ± 4 months.

Also known as Livingstone's Antelope.

♂

♀

Mass 4,3–5,5 kg.

Length of horns **Average** ± 8 cm. **Record** 10,48 cm.

Food Mainly leaves, but also fresh grass shoots.

Life expectancy ± 9 years.

Enemies Leopard, lion, caracal.

2–2,5 cm

Damara Dik-dik

Damara Dik-dik
Madoqua kirkii

Description The colour is usually a finely speckled grey-brown on the back and buttocks, while the neck, shoulders and flanks are a lighter brown. The chest, belly and the area around the eyes are almost white. The horns rise just behind the eyes and slope backwards in line with the face. Between the horns and on the forehead is a distinguishing tuft of long hair which can be raised. The upper lip is longer than the lower lip.

Sexual dimorphism Only the males are horned.

Habitat Dense woodland with shrubs and little grass. Not dependent on water.

Habits Damara Dik-dik occur singly or in groups of two or three. Small groups of up to six are also seen in dry months. They browse very early in the morning and late in the afternoon, sometimes until after dusk. During the heat of day they rest in dense shade. They always use communal manure heaps. When alarmed, they may run with stiff legs, bouncing away and emitting a loud whistle each time their feet touch the ground.

Voice A high-pitched quivering whistle and a short, explosive whistle when disturbed.

Breeding A single lamb is born from December to April after a gestation period of 5½ to 6 months.

♂

♀

| Mass | ♂ 15–21 kg. |
| | ♀ 17–25 kg. |

Length of horns
Average ± 11 cm.
Record 18,1 cm.

Food Mainly leaves, but also shoots, flowers, fruit and seeds.

Life expectancy
± 10 years.

Enemies Leopard, caracal, African wild dog, lion.

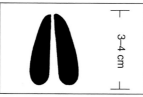

3–4 cm

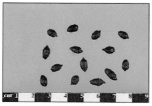

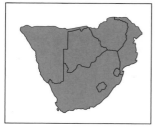

Grey Duiker

Duiker
Sylvicapra grimmia

Description The colour of this small antelope varies from yellowish-grey-brown to reddish-yellow-brown with fine speckles. The belly and the insides of the limbs are white. There is a tuft of long, black hair between the horns. The black stripe from the forehead to the nose is characteristic. There are also dark stripes on the front of the forelegs. The dark tail is narrow, short and white underneath. The Grey Duiker differs from the Red Duiker by its larger build and greyish colour.

Sexual dimorphism Females are slightly larger than males and lack horns.

Habitat Areas with enough bush and undergrowth for shade and shelter.

Habits Grey Duiker are usually solitary but form pairs during the mating season. They graze or browse early in the morning, late in the afternoon and sometimes at night. They rest in thick shelter during the heat of the day. They will lie quietly and wait until danger is almost upon them before jumping up. When they run they dip their heads and use characteristic jumping, turning and swerving movements. They still occur outside conservation areas, but are then more nocturnal.

Voice Snort and a nasal alarm call.

Breeding 1, occasionally 2, lambs are born any time of the year after a gestation period of ± 3 months.

Also known as Common Duiker.

♂

♀

Mass	♂ 10–14 kg.
	♀ 11–14 kg.

Length of horns
Average ± 6 cm.
Record 11,43 cm.

Food Leaves, wild fruit and young shoots. They regularly drink water.

Life expectancy
± 12 years.

Enemies Leopard, lion, caracal, python.

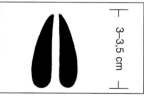

3–3,5 cm

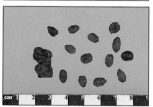

Red Duiker

Rooiduiker
Cephalophus natalensis

Description The general colour is chestnut to reddish-brown while the belly is slightly lighter. There is a tuft of darker hair between the horns, and the throat and insides of the ears are white. The ears are short and rounded with a black margin. The tail darkens towards the tip and ends in white. Both sexes have short, straight horns which lie slightly backwards in line with the face.

Sexual dimorphism None.

Habitat Moist riverine bush, mountain bush, thickets in rocky areas and coastal forest, with sufficient water.

Habits Red Duiker are solitary animals, sometimes found in temporary pairs or small groups. They are shy, mainly nocturnal animals and are seldom seen except on cooler, overcast days. They are fond of grazing under trees where monkeys drop wild fruit. When alarmed they immediately take cover in thick bush. Red Duiker use communal manure heaps.

Voice A loud "che-che" whistle when they run away and a whistle-like scream.

Breeding A single lamb is born any time of the year.

Also known as Natal Duiker.

Burger Cillié

♀

Burger Cillié

♂

Mass ♂ 3,8–5,5 kg.
♀ 4,6–7,3 kg.

Length of horns
Average ± 3 cm.
Record 7,30 cm.

Food Mainly leaves, but also wild fruit and young branches. They drink water regularly.

Life expectancy
± 7 years.

Enemies Leopard, python.

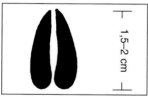

1,5–2 cm

Blue Duiker

Blouduiker
Philantomba monticola

Description The Blue Duiker is our smallest antelope. The colour varies from dark reddish-brown to dark greyish-brown and is darker on the back with a bluish sheen. Colouring is lighter on the belly and on the throat and chest. The cheeks and areas around the eyes are light brown in colour with two horizontal black stripes extending from below the eyes towards the nose. The tail is white underneath and has a white edge. Both sexes have short horns which slope backwards in line with the face.

Sexual dimorphism Males have a slightly smaller build than females.

Habitat Limited to forests, thickets and coastal bush.

Habits Blue Duiker are usually solitary but are also found in pairs. They are very shy and will, at the slightest disturbance, flee to shelter in the thick undergrowth. They usually browse in the early morning or late afternoon and even at night. They come out to the more open areas on the edge of the forest at night. By day they are very alert and cautiously approach open spots.

Voice A sharp alarm whistle.

Breeding A single lamb is born any time of the year after a gestation period of ± 4 months.

♂

Nigel Dennis/Gallo

♀

Burger Cillié

| Mass | ♂ ± 70 kg. |
| | ♀ ± 61 kg. |

Length of horns
Average ± 38 cm.
Record 52,39 cm.

Food Exclusively grass, especially short grass.

Life expectancy
± 11 years.

Enemy Cheetah.

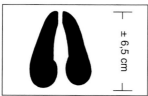

± 6,5 cm

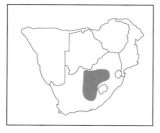

Blesbok

Blesbok
Damaliscus pygargus phillipsi

Description The neck and the top of the back are brown. Lower down on the flanks and buttocks the colouring becomes darker. The belly, the inside of the buttocks and the area up to the base of the tail are white. The small blaze above the eyes and the larger blaze on the face are usually seperated at eye-level. The lambs are a much lighter brown. Both sexes have horns. The Blesbok differs from the Bontebok by having less white on the coat and with the blaze on the face usually separated.

Sexual dimorphism Females have a slighter build than males.

Habitat Open plains of the South African highveld.

Habits Blesbok form herds consisting of females and juveniles. Males are solitary. They graze in the morning and late in the afternoon, resting during the heat of day. During the mating season the territorial males will collect a herd of females which pass through their areas and court them. Serious fights occur between the males, but after the mating season the territorial activities decrease. Sometimes the males lie on heaps of manure to rest. Blesbok have the habit of walking in single file.

Voice Snort and growl.

Breeding A single young is born from November to January after a gestation period of ± 8 months.

♂

Burger Cillié

♀

Heindrich van der Berg

| Mass | ♂ ± 64 kg. |
| | ♀ ± 59 kg. |

Length of horns
Average ± 38 cm.
Record 42,55 cm.

Food Exclusively grass, especially short grass.

Life expectancy
± 11 years.

Enemy Leopard.

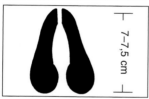
7-7,5 cm

Bontebok

Bontebok
Damaliscus pygargus dorcas

Description This is a colourful animal with the brown colouring in some places shading to dark brown and black with a purple sheen. The belly, the area inside of the buttocks, a patch around the crop and the lower legs are white. Both sexes have horns. The small blaze above the eyes and the larger blaze on the face usually merge. The Bontebok can be distinguished from the Blesbok by the larger white patches on the body, especially the white patch around the crop.

Sexual dimorphism Females have thinner horns and are slightly smaller than males.

Habitat Open grassy plains in fynbos with sufficient water.

Habits Bontebok form herds of separate sexes. Some males are territorial and are solitary. If a female herd passes through a male's area in the mating season, it will round them up and court them. Territorial males use the same manure heap and sometimes lie down on top of it. They usually graze early in the morning and late in the afternoon, resting during the heat of the day. They were an endangered species but their survival is now assured in the Bontebok Park near Swellendam from where surplus stock is translocated to other areas.

Voice Growl and snort.

Breeding A single young is born from September to November after a gestation period of ± 8 months.

♂

Burger Cillié

♀

Ulrich Oberprieler

Mass	♂ 140 kg.
	♀ 126 kg.

Length of horns
Average ± 34 cm.
Record 46,99 cm.

Food They select palatable grass and are dependent on water.

Life expectancy ± 15 years.

Enemies Spotted hyaena, cheetah, leopard, lion, African wild dog.

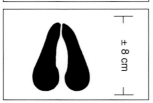

± 8 cm

Tsessebe

Basterhartbees
Damaliscus lunatus

Description The colouring is dark reddish-brown with a metallic sheen. The blaze on the face as well as the upper parts of the forelegs and hind legs down to the knees are black. Below the knees the colour is light brown. The animal has a hump on the shoulders and the back characteristically slopes downwards. Both sexes have horns. The Tsessebe differs from the Red Hartebeest in that it is not as red and the horns are shorter and set more widely apart. Lichtenstein's Hartebeest lacks the black blaze on the face of the Tsessebe.

Sexual dimorphism Females are smaller than males.

Habitat Open savannah and grassy plains in surrounding woodland with medium to tall grass and sufficient water.

Habits Tsessebe are gregarious and are usually found in small breeding herds, bachelor groups or family herds. Territorial males are solitary. During the winter these animals herd together more often. They are very inquisitive and usually run away for only a short distance and then stop to look back. Tsessebe are the fastest runners of all the antelope in the region. They are fond of horning the ground, especially after rain. They are sometimes found together with Zebra or Blue Wildebeest.

Voice Snort.

Breeding A single calf is born from September to November after a gestation period of ± 8 months.

Also known as Sassaby.

Mass ♂	137–180 kg.
♀	105–136 kg.

Length of horns
Average ± 52 cm.
Record 74,93 cm.

Food Exclusively grass, especially red grass. Can go long periods without water.

Life expectancy
± 13 years.

Enemies Spotted hyaena, leopard, lion, African wild dog.

± 8,5 cm

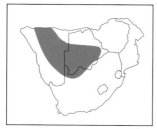

Red Hartebeest

Rooihartbees
Alcelaphus buselaphus

Description This hartebeest has peculiarly shaped horns and a long face. The colour is a glossy reddish-brown. The blaze on the face, the tail and the outside of the legs are black, while the buttocks are light brown at the back. The shoulders are high and humped and the back slopes downwards. The Red Hartebeest can be distinguished from Lichtenstein's Hartebeest by the reddish-brown colouring, the black blaze on the face and the black legs. The horns of the Tsessebe have a different shape and their colouring is not as reddish-brown.

Sexual dimorphism Females are smaller than males.

Habitat Open areas or grassy plains in dry savannah and semi-arid areas.

Habits They form herds of 10 to 20 animals or in some cases up to a few hundred. Old males are solitary or form small herds. Other herds consist of females and young with a male as leader. They usually graze early in the morning and late in the afternoon. They have an acute sense of smell and hearing but their eyesight is poor. They can run very fast, galloping gracefully. They are very inquisitive – they will run a short distance, stop and look back, and may even come closer again.

Voice A warning sneezing-snort.

Breeding A single calf is born from October to December after a gestation period of ± 8 months.

Also known as Cape Hartebeest.

Burger Cillié

♂

Burger Cillié

♀

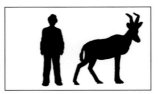

| Mass | ♂ 157–204 kg. |
| | ♀ 160–181 kg. |

Length of horns
Average ± 52 cm.
Record 61,91 cm.

Food Fresh, sprouting green grass and sometimes leaves. They drink water regularly.

Life expectancy
Unknown.

Enemies Spotted hyaena, leopard, lion, African wild dog.

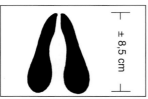

± 8,5 cm

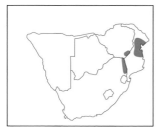

Lichtenstein's Hartebeest

Mofhartbees
Alcelaphus lichtensteinii

Description The animal is dull yellow-brown or chestnut with the buttocks around the tail a lighter colour. The tuft of hair on the tail and the shins are black. Both sexes are horned. Black patches are sometimes seen just behind the shoulders. These are caused when the animal rubs its horns and the sides of the face after it has horned the ground or grazed on burnt tufts of grass. Lichtenstein's Hartebeest differs from the Red Hartebeest by having a lighter colour. It also lacks the black blaze on the face and the high pedicel which carries the horns.

Sexual dimorphism Females are slightly smaller than males.

Habitat Areas between vleis and the surrounding woodland or dry floodplains.

Habits Lichtenstein's Hartebeest form herds of 3 to 15 animals consisting of a dominant male, females and juveniles. Other males are solitary or form small herds. They rest during the heat of day and graze when it is cooler. They have an acute sense of sight but a poor sense of smell. The males stand on top of anthills to survey the vicinity for any danger – this is probably the main reason why they were hunted to extinction in South Africa. During 1985 they were reintroduced into the Kruger National Park.

Voice Bellow or a sneezing snort.

Breeding A single calf is born from June to September after a gestation period of ± 8 months.

♂

♀

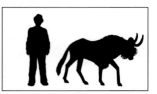

Mass	♂ ± 180 kg.
	♀ ± 140 kg.

Length of horns
Average ± 52 cm.
Record 74,61 cm.

Food Mainly grass and sometimes karoo bush.

Life expectancy
± 20 years.

Enemies None.

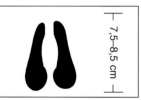

7,5–8,5 cm

Black Wildebeest

Swartwildebees
Connochaetes gnou

Description An ox-like animal with unusual horns, a beard and hair on the nose. The colouring is dark brown and the horse-like tail is almost white. The calves are a uniform light brown colour. The back slopes downwards. Both sexes have horns. The Black Wildebeest can be distinguished from the Blue Wildebeest by its conspicuous white tail, smaller build and horns which curve forward.

Sexual dimorphism Females are smaller than males.

Habitat Open grassland with sufficient water.

Habits These animals occur naturally only in South Africa. They form herds of 6 to about 50 individuals consisting of adult males, females and juveniles, or adult males only. They usually graze in the early morning or late afternoon, resting at midday. In cold weather they graze at any time. Sometimes they are seen kneeling while they feed. During the mating season males are very aggressive when they protect their territories but serious fights seldom occur.

Voice A loud snorting bellow and "ghe-nu" sound by territorial males.

Breeding A single calf is born from November to December after a gestation period of ± 8½ months.

Also known as White-tailed Gnu.

HPH Photography

Burger Cillié

| Mass | ♂ 230–270 kg. |
| | ♀ 160–200 kg. |

Length of horns
Average ± 60 cm.
Record 86,04 cm.

Food Short grass, 15 cm or shorter.

Life expectancy
± 20 years.

Enemies Spotted hyaena, cheetah, leopard, lion, African wild dog.

9,5–10 cm

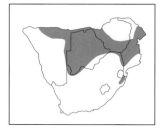

Blue Wildebeest

Blouwildebees
Connochaetes taurinus

Description This ox-like animal is a dark grey-brown with darker vertical stripes on the neck and flanks. The face, mane, beard, throat hairs and long horse-like tail are black. The calf has a light reddish-brown colour and short erect horns. The back slopes downwards. Both males and females have horns. The Blue Wildebeest can be distinguished from the Black Wildebeest by its larger size and distribution – it does not occur on the grass plains of the Highveld. In addition, the Black Wildebeest's horns curve forward and the tail is white.

Sexual dimorphism Females are considerably smaller than males.

Habitat Open bushveld with plenty of shortish grass and sufficient water.

Habits Blue Wildebeest are gregarious, diurnal animals. The herd of 20 to 30 animals consists mainly of females and young, with a male as leader. Bachelor herds and very large herds also occur. These animals prefer to graze while it is cool and rest at midday. They move seasonally in search of good grazing when the grass becomes too tall. They often mingle socially with Plains Zebras which graze on taller grass. During the mating season the males mark out a certain territory for themselves.

Voice Snort and bellow. Young ones bleat or make a "hunn" noise.

Breeding 1, seldom 2, calves are born from November to February after a gestation period of ± 8½ months.

Also known as Brindled Gnu.

♂

♀

Burger Cillié

Burger Cillié

Mass	♂ 750–820 kg.
	♀ 680–750 kg.

Length of horns
Average ± 100 cm.
Record 162,56 cm.

Food Grass, but sometimes shoots and leaves as well. They drink water regularly.

Life expectancy
± 23 years.

Enemy Lion.

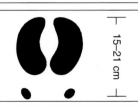

15–21 cm

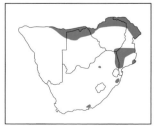

African Buffalo

Buffel
Syncerus caffer

Description Large cattle-like animals. The colour of the juvenile is light reddish-brown, the male darkening with age until it is a grey-black colour. The mature male is darker than the female which retains a reddish-brown tinge. These animals are fond of wallowing in mud and consequently take on the colour of the soil. Both sexes are horned, while the horns of the male are especially large with broad, thick bosses. The ears are situated below the horns.

Sexual dimorphism Males are more heavily built and have larger and heavier horns than females.

Habitat Savannah with sufficient edible grass and shade, usually near water.

Habits African Buffalo are diurnal animals living in herds of up to several hundred. Old males are solitary or form small herds. They usually graze at night or during the cooler parts of the day and like to sleep on bare patches of ground. During summer they may move away from permanent water in search of new grazing areas. They are inquisitive animals with an acute sense of smell but poor eyesight and hearing. They are known to be one of the most dangerous of animals to hunt, because when wounded, they circle back and wait for a chance to attack the hunter.

Voice A cattle-like bellow.

Breeding A single calf is born from August to February after a gestation period of ± 11 months.

♂

Burger Cillié

♀

Duncan Butchart/African Images

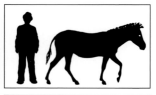

Mass ♂ 290–340 kg.
♀ 290–325 kg.

Food Grass, occasionally leaves and pods as well.

Life expectancy
± 35 years.

Enemies Spotted hyaena, lion, cheetah.

10,5–11,5 cm

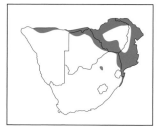

Plains Zebra

Vlaktekwagga
Equus quagga

Description The Plains Zebra is now the same species as the extinct Quagga, which means that the Quagga was never really extinct and the old Burchell's Zebra is now a Quagga! The body of this horse-like animal is white with dark stripes alternating with lighter shadow stripes. Each individual has its own pattern of stripes. The colour of the stripes becomes less distinct towards the hooves. Plains Zebra can be distinguished from the Cape Mountain Zebra by its shadow stripes, longer mane and smaller ears. It also does not have a dewlap or a white belly.

Sexual dimorphism Males are usually slightly heavier than females.

Habitat Open savannah with grass and sufficient water.

Habits Plains Zebras form family herds of 4 to 9 animals, each herd usually consisting of a male, a few females and some young. Other males are solitary or form stallion herds. They are diurnal animals which range seasonally over large areas in search of food. Their senses are acute and they enjoy a dust-bath. Plains Zebras are often seen socially with Blue Wildebeest. A male will protect its herd, or a female and her foal, by biting and kicking.

Voice A repetitive "qua-ha-ha" whinny followed by a whistling sound as they inhale air.

Breeding A single foal is born any time of the year after a gestation period of ± 12½ months, peaking in summer.

Also known as Burchell's Zebra.

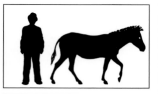

Mass	♂ 250–260 kg.
	♀ 204–257 kg.

Food Grass and occasionally leaves.

Life expectancy ± 35 years.

Enemies None.

± 10 cm

Cape Mountain Zebra

Kaapse Bergkwagga
Equus zebra zebra

Description This animal is white with black stripes, which end in a horizontal line low down on the flanks, leaving the belly white. The stripes extend the full length of the legs to the hooves. Just behind the black nose there is an orange suffusion. The Cape Mountain Zebra can be distinguished from Plains Zebra by its dewlap and white belly. It also lacks the shadow stripes of Plains Zebra. Hartmann's Mountain Zebra is more heavily built and the stripes on the buttocks are usually narrower than those of the Cape Mountain Zebra.

Sexual dimorphism Males are usually larger than females.

Habitat Restricted to mountainous areas with sufficient water for drinking and grazing.

Habits Cape Mountain Zebras are gregarious animals. Herds consist of a male, females and young animals. Other males are solitary or form bachelor herds. Members of the family group usually stay with the same herd for life. They are active early in the morning and in the late afternoon. They rest for the remainder of the day, but not necessarily in the shade. They are very fond of dust-baths. If a young male challenges an older one, it leads to a fight in which they bite and kick each other.

Voice A snort or a high-pitched alarm call when they are threatened.

Breeding A single foal is born any time of the year after a gestation period of ± 12 months.

♂

Niel Cillié

♀

Burger Cillié

Mass ♂ 270–330 kg.	
♀ 250–300 kg.	

Food Grass, occasionally small branches and shrubs.

Life expectancy
± 35 years.

Enemies Spotted hyaena, lion, cheetah.

± 11 cm

Hartmann's Mountain Zebra

Hartmannse Bergkwagga
Equus zebra hartmannae

Description The black stripes of this zebra are clearly visible against the yellowish-white background. The legs are striped up to the hooves. Some distance down the flanks the stripes end, leaving the belly white. The dewlap as well as the orange suffusion above the snout are evident. Hartmann's Mountain Zebra differs from Plains Zebra in that it has a dewlap and a white belly, and lacks shadow stripes. It is more heavily built than the Cape Mountain Zebra and the stripes on the buttocks are usually narrower.

Sexual dimorphism Males have a slightly heavier build than females.

Habitat Stony and mountainous slopes with sufficient grazing and drinking water.

Habits Hartmann's Zebras are gregarious animals, forming herds which consist of a dominant male and his family group. Other males form bachelor herds. The family group is stable and an individual will usually remain with the same herd for life. These animals generally graze during the cooler parts of the day and rest in the shade at midday. They are very fond of dust-baths. Fights between males consist of biting and kicking.

Voice Snorting and a shrill alarm call.

Breeding A single foal is born any time of the year (peaking in summer), after a gestation period of ± 12 months.

Mass ♂ 60–100 kg.
♀ 45–70 kg.

Length of teeth
Average ± 20 cm.
Record 60,96 cm.

Food Grass and fallen wild fruit, also succulent roots.

Life expectancy
± 20 years.

Enemies Lion, leopard, African wild dog.

3,5–4,5 cm

Common Warthog

Vlakvark
Phacochoerus africanus

Description The Common Warthog has distinctive white whiskers and warts on the sides of the face. The grey body is sparsely covered with long bristles and there is a mane of dark hair with lighter tips. The tip of the tail has a small tuft of black hair. The adult has long tusks which curve over a broad snout. This animal is seen more often than the Bushpig from which it is distinguished by the broader snout, long curved tusks and more prominent warts on the face. It is also grey, not dark brown like the Bushpig.

Sexual dimorphism Males are large and have two pairs of warts and long tusks. The females' tusks are shorter and they have only one pair of warts.

Habitat Savannah with open areas around pans and waterholes.

Habits Warthogs are diurnal and form family or bachelor groups of 4 to 10 animals. They are sometimes solitary. They live in old antbear holes, entering backwards and emerging head first. They are able to defend themselves against cheetahs and wild dogs, but not against lions. They are fond of digging in the soil or mud-bathing, taking up the colour of the soil. When they run, they characteristically hold their tails erect. They kneel down on their front legs to root and graze.

Voice Growl, grunt and snort.

Breeding 1 to 8 young are born from September to December after a gestation period of ± 5½ months.

Also known as Warthog.

♂

Burger Cillié

♀

Burger Cillié

Mass ♂ 46–82 kg.
♀ 48–66 kg.

Length of teeth
Average ± 11 cm.
Record 30,16 cm.

Food Rhizomes, bulbs and tubers and will eat vegetables and fruit.

Life expectancy
± 20 years.

Enemy Leopard.

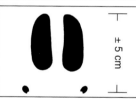

± 5 cm

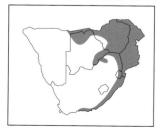

Bushpig

Bosvark
Potamochoerus larvatus

Description A very hairy animal that resembles the domestic pig. The colour varies from grey-brown to dark brown, becoming darker with age. The mane, which bristles when the animal is agitated, is a lighter colour. The upper parts of the face are lighter in colour while the lower portions of the legs are black. The sharp tusks are not very long. The young have distinct white horizontal stripes on the body. Bushpigs are browner than the Warthog and usually lick the warts on the face. They also have smaller tusks, a narrower snout and more pointed ears.

Sexual dimorphism Males are usually slightly larger than females.

Habitat They frequent thickets, riverine underbush and reedbeds close to water.

Habits Bushpigs form groups of 6 to 12 animals consisting of a dominant male, a dominant female, other females and juveniles. They are nocturnal and are seldom seen during daytime as they usually rest in thick shelter. Small groups with young are always aggressive. Bushpigs are dangerous when wounded. They are good swimmers and like to wallow in cooling mud. Like Warthogs, they are fond of digging in the soil.

Voice The alarm call is a long, resonant growl and they grunt softly when foraging.

Breeding 3 to 8 young are born from November to January after a gestation period of ± 4 months.

Warwick Tarboton/Gallo

♂

Anthony Bannister/Gallo

♀

Mass ♂ 970–1 395 kg.
♀ 700–950 kg.

Food Mainly leaves but also grass.

Life expectancy ± 28 years.

Enemies Spotted hyaena, cheetah, leopard, lion.

± 19 cm

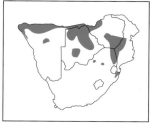

Giraffe

Kameelperd
Giraffa camelopardalis

Description Giraffes are characterised by their long legs and very long neck, which has seven cervical vertebrae – the same number as humans. The background colour is whitish-yellow covered with patches of light brown which become darker with age. On top of the head are two short horns, the tops of which are covered with black hair. There are no dark patches on the upper part of the muzzle and on the forehead. They have a mane of short, stiff hair.

Sexual dimorphism Females usually have a slighter build than males.

Habitat Open woodland to shrubby, dry savannah. Several different acacia types are a requirement of their diet.

Habits Giraffes are diurnal animals which live in herds with a fairly loose structure, individuals moving between the herds as they please. Males are usually solitary. They usually rest during the hottest part of the day. As they walk, the legs on the same side swing simultaneously. Although they appear clumsy, they can gallop surprisingly fast. Females with calves defend themselves against lions and can even kill them. Males fight by swinging at and hitting each other with their necks and heads.

Voice Grunt or snort, if alarmed.

Breeding A single calf is born any time of the year after a gestation period of ± 15 months.

♂

Burger Cillié

♀ + ♀

Burger Cillié

Top – Black Rhino (Ulrich Oberprieler), Right – Elephant's eye (Eric Reisinger)

Very Large Mammals

Very large browsers

and grazers with

bare greyish skin

and large feet.

| Mass | ♂ 5 500–6 000 kg. |
| | ♀ 3 600–4 000 kg. |

Tusk
Record mass 102,7 kg.
Record length 3,48 m.

Food Grass, bark of trees, leaved branches, and fruit.

Life expectancy
± 65 years.

Enemy Lion.

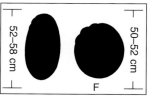

52–58 cm   50–52 cm   F

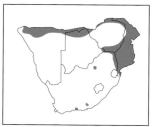

African Elephant

Olifant
Loxodonta africana

Description A huge, heavily built animal with long, stout legs and large feet. The colour is brownish-grey and sometimes matches the ground colour of its habitat. Although the skin is hairless, the tip of the tail consists of long hair. This animal is characterised by its large flat ears, a trunk, and tusks, which vary in length. The trunk serves as a nose and is also used for breaking off branches, for transferring all manner of vegetation to the mouth, and for siphoning up water for showering itself or for squirting into the mouth.

Sexual dimorphism Females are smaller than males and have smaller tusks.

Habitat Very adaptable, but they prefer areas providing enough grass and leafy vegetation and clean drinking water.

Habits African Elephants are diurnal and nocturnal, forming herds of 6 to approximately 200 animals, with a cow as herd leader. Old males form small bachelor herds, but are sometimes solitary. African Elephants range widely in search of food. They are normally peaceful but can be dangerous, especially when they have calves or when wounded. They are not fond of sharing drinking places with other animals and may chase them away. They swim well and enjoy wallowing in mud. They have a strong sense of smell, but their hearing and sight are poor.

Voice Trumpeting and a belly rumbling.

Breeding 1, exceptionally 2, calves are born any time of the year after a gestation period of ± 22 months.

Also known as Elephant.

♂

♀

Mass ♂ 2 000–2 300 kg.   ♀ 1 400–1 600 kg.

Length of horn   **Average** ± 85 cm.   **Record** 158,12 cm.

Food Grass, preferring short grass.

Life expectancy   ± 45 years.

Enemy Lion.

28–30 cm

White Rhinoceros

Witrenoster
Ceratotherium simum

Description The larger of the two rhinoceroses. It is prehistoric in appearance with a barrel-shaped body and a long head with two horns on the snout. The horns consist of tubular, filament hair-like outgrowths, the front horn being longer than the rear horn. The square lips are characteristic. The colour is grey but sometimes matches the ground colour of its habitat. The ears are pointed. The Black Rhinoceros has a pointed upper lip and is smaller, walking with the head held higher from the ground.

Sexual dimorphism Females are lighter in build than males.

Habitat Open and bushy savannah with patches of short grass, sufficient drinking water and trees and thickets for cover.

Habits These animals live in small groups consisting of a territorial male, other males, females and juveniles. Territorial males demarcate their territories by manure heaps and spray-urinating. They are restricted to their home range, not wandering far afield. Although they appear clumsy, they can run surprisingly fast. Calves usually walk in front of their mothers. Rhinoceros' eyesight is poor but they have an acute sense of smell and hearing. They are fond of wallowing in mud when it is hot and are not as aggressive as the Black Rhinoceros.

Voice Snort, puff and growl.

Breeding A single calf is born any time of the year after a gestation period of ± 16 months.

Also known as Square-lipped Rhinoceros.

♂

Burger Cillié

♀

Duncan Butchart/African Images

| Mass | ♂ 730–970 kg. |
| | ♀ 760–1 000 kg. |

Length of horn
Average ± 78 cm.
Record 135,89 cm.

Food Leaves, branches and thorns.

Life expectancy ± 40 years.

Enemy Lion.

22–24 cm

Black Rhinoceros

Swartrenoster
Diceros bicornis

Description The smaller of the rhinoceroses. It has a barrel-shaped body and long head with two horns on the snout. The horns consist of tubular, filament hair-like outgrowths. The ears are small and rounded. The upper lip is pointed and prehensile. The colour is dark grey but sometimes matches the ground colour of its habitat. The Black Rhinoceros is distinguished from the White Rhinoceros by its pointed upper lip, shorter head and smaller build, and the absence of the hump above the shoulders. When it walks it usually holds its head higher than the White Rhinoceros does.

Sexual dimorphism Males are slightly lighter in build than females.

Habitat Dense shrubby and treed areas with plenty of water.

Habits These animals are usually solitary. A cow and her calf are also seen together, the calf usually walking behind its mother. They are fond of mud-baths and rest in shady areas when it is hot. Their eyesight is poor but the senses of smell and hearing are acute. They browse early in the morning or late afternoon and drink water in the evening. Males avoid contact with each other and may fight to death. Black Rhinoceroses are sometimes moody and charge blindly, often just to ascertain whether an object poses any danger.

Voice A snort which is repeated. They also growl and scream.

Breeding A single calf is born any time of the year after a gestation period of ± 15 months.

Also known as Hook-lipped Rhinoceros.

♂

♀

| Mass | ♂ 970–2 000 kg. |
| | ♀ 995–1 675 kg. |

Length of canine
Average ± 60 cm.
Record 163,83 cm.

Food Grass – up to 130 kg each night.

Life expectancy ± 39 years.

Enemy Lion.

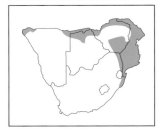

Hippopotamus

Seekoei
Hippopotamus amphibius

Description A very large, distinctive aquatic animal. The general colour is grey-brown but the belly and skin folds are yellowish-pink. The skin is virtually bare. It has short legs and is stockily built. The mouth is very large and the eyes are situated on top of the head. The animal usually lies submerged in the water with only the nose, eyes and ears protruding. The erect ears are small in relation to the head and the tail is short and flattened.

Sexual dimorphism Males are larger than females.

Habitat Stretches of open permanent water in which they can submerge and sandbanks with sufficient food in the surrounding areas.

Habits These gregarious animals form schools of 6 to 15 members with a female leader. They feed at night and rest during the day, submerged in the water, or otherwise bask on sandbanks. In the late afternoon they begin to come out of the water to feed. Sometimes they feed several kilometres from water, especially during times of drought. They often use the same route, eventually trampling it into a wide double path. Although they are generally placid animals they can be aggressive and even very dangerous at times – this is especially true of cows with calves.

Voice A mixture between a loud, high-pitched roar and a bellow, followed by approximately five successive lower-pitched, short calls.

Breeding A single calf is born any time of the year after a gestation period of 7 to 8 months.

♂

Duncan Butchart/African Images

♀

Burger Cillié

Top – Leopard (Richard du Toit), Right – Lion (Eric Reisinger)

Carnivores

Cat- and dog-like

animals that hunt

or are scavengers.

Mass	♂ 180–240 kg.
	♀ 120–180 kg.

Food Mainly hoofed animals.

Life expectancy ± 20 years.

Enemy Crocodile.

12,5–15,5 cm

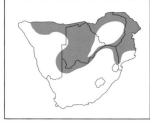

Lion

Leeu
Panthera leo

Description These tawny animals are the largest of Africa's cat family. The young have characteristic rosettes and spots which usually disappear as the animal matures. Males usually have manes, some darker than others. The Lion has a white beard and long, white whiskers growing from dark spots on the upper lip. The back of the ears is black, and the tail ends in a tuft of black hair. The large paws are padded and have well-developed claws.

Sexual dimorphism Males are often maned and are much larger than females.

Habitat Lions are very adaptable and occur in most types of habitat where there is enough food.

Habits Lions are the only social cats and form small prides of 3 to 12 animals – as many as 30 have been seen together. They are mainly nocturnal and generally sleep during the day, but are often seen at dawn and dusk. The pride consists of one, or occasionally more than one, dominant male, a dominant female, mature and young animals.

Hunting habits The lionesses usually hunt in a group: stalking their prey against the wind, trying to come as close as possible, before they pounce upon it.

Voice The well-known "uuuuh-huumph" sound which starts high and ends lower, is repeated at intervals and becomes softer until it ends in a few groans.

Breeding 1 to 4 (exceptionally up to 6) cubs are born any time of the year after a gestation period of ± 3½ months.

♂

♀

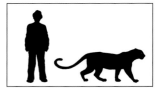

Mass ♂ 20–82 kg.
♀ 17–35 kg.

Food From small animals such as mice and hyraxes to medium-sized antelope.

Life expectancy ± 20 years.

Enemies Lion, crocodile.

9–10 cm

Leopard

Luiperd
Panthera pardus

Description Colouring varies from white to bright golden-brown, with black spots and rosettes. The rosettes consist of groups of 4 to 6 spots arranged in a tight ring. The tail exceeds half the body length measured from head to tail. This cat has small, round ears and long whiskers growing from dark spots on the upper lip. The size of the Leopard varies considerably in the region. It differs from the Cheetah in having shorter legs and rosette-like instead of solid spots. It also lacks the Cheetah's black tear marks from eye to mouth.

Sexual dimorphism Females are smaller than males.

Habitat Mostly in or near thickets on mountain sides, or along streams and rivers.

Habits Although leopards are mainly nocturnal, they are also seen during the day, especially in the early mornings and late afternoons. They are usually alone, except in the mating season. They are shy, cunning and dangerous, especially when wounded. Leopards are very good tree climbers and can pull fairly large prey up a tree to protect it, during their absence, from other predators or scavengers in the vicinity. They return later to feed again. Leopards' senses are well developed. They still occur outside conservation areas.

Hunting habits They stalk and pounce upon their prey, making use of stealth and cover in their approach.

Voice A "sawing" sound and a hoarse cough, but other sounds are also made.

Breeding 2 to 3 (exceptionally up to 6) cubs are born any time of the year after a gestation period of ± 3 months.

Mass ♂ 39–60 kg.
♀ 36–48 kg.

Food Small to medium-sized antelope, ostriches, warthogs, hares and guinea fowl.

Life expectancy
± 12 years.

Enemies Lion, crocodile.

8,5–11,5 cm

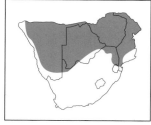

Cheetah

Jagluiperd
Acinonyx jubatus

Description An elegant, slender cat with long legs. The colour is buffy-white with black spots. The belly, chin and throat are white, with smaller black spots on the chest. The spots on the tail are replaced by black rings towards the tip. The ears are small, round and set far apart. The Cheetah is distinguished from the Leopard by its longer legs, black spots on the body and the characteristic tear marks extending from the eyes to the mouth.

Sexual dimorphism Females have a slighter build than males.

Habitat Open woodland and savannah.

Habits Cheetahs are usually found in pairs, although individuals, small groups, or females with their young have been seen. They are diurnal and most active at sunrise and sunset. During the hottest part of the day they rest in the shade of trees. Cheetahs are the fastest of all animals, reaching a speed of 100 km/h and more over short distances. They are not aggressive although they sometimes paw and bite at each other.

Hunting habits They usually hunt alone, except when they hunt larger animals, relying on speed to overtake their prey.

Voice A high, bird-like whistle.

Breeding 1 to 5 young are born any time of the year after a gestation period of ± 3 months.

Mass	♂ 8,6–20,0 kg. ♀ 4,2–14,5 kg.

Food Small mammals, birds and reptiles.

Life expectancy ± 11 years.

Enemies Lion, crocodile.

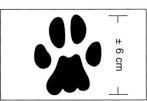

± 6 cm

Caracal

Rooikat
Caracal caracal

Description The Caracal is a well-built animal with strong legs, remarkably large paws and a relatively short tail. The colour is light reddish-brown to brick-red, sometimes speckled with silver. The belly and chest are white. There are dark spots above and on the inner corners of the eyes and at the base of the whiskers. There are black tassels of hair on the tips of the ears. The paws are a dull yellow-white. The size of the animal varies considerably in the region.

Sexual dimorphism Females have a slighter build than males.

Habitat Very adaptable. They usually prefer savannah or open patches in woody country.

Habits Caracals are mainly nocturnal but can also be seen during daytime, especially in the early mornings and in the late afternoons. Although good tree climbers, they are predominantly terrestrial. They rest during the heat of day, camouflaging themselves effectively even in little shelter. They hunt alone.

Voice Purr and a "chirp" like a bird.

Breeding 2 to 4 (exceptionally 5) cubs are born from October to March after a gestation period of ± 2 months.

Also known as Lynx.

Mass	♂ 8,6–13,5 kg.
	♀ 8,6–11,8 kg.

Food Small mammals, such as cane rats, hares, mice and sometimes birds.

Life expectancy ± 12 years.

Enemies Lion, crocodile.

± 5 cm

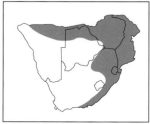

Serval

Tierboskat
Leptailurus serval

Description The Serval is a slender animal with long legs, a rather small, rounded head and large ears. The colour varies from dull white to light golden-yellow with black stripes down the neck and irregular black spots on the body. The rather short tail is spotted from the base, merging into black rings and ending in a black tip. The belly and the insides of the legs are white with dark spots. There are two black stripes on white behind the ears. The Serval may be confused with a young Cheetah, but has larger ears and lacks the Cheetah's characteristic tear marks.

Sexual dimorphism Females have a slighter build than males.

Habitat Servals prefer thicker, more humid types of woodland with sufficient shelter and water.

Habits These animals usually forage alone, although pairs sometimes hunt together, even in swampy areas. They are mainly nocturnal but can also be seen early in the morning and late in the afternoon. They can run very fast for short distances. At night they range far in search of food, using roads or footpaths to avoid difficult terrain. Although they are good tree climbers, they are mainly terrestrial.

Voice A repeated high-pitched call to partner. Snarls, growls and spits in anger.

Breeding 1 to 4 young are born from September to April after a gestation period of ± 2 months.

Wim Vorster

Roger de la Harpe/KZN Parks

Mass ♂ 3,8–6,4 kg.
♀ 2,6–5,5 kg.

Food Mice and marsh rats, also birds, insects, smaller mammals, spiders and fruit.

Life expectancy
Unknown.

Enemies Leopard, lion.

± 3,5 cm

African Wild Cat

Vaalboskat
Felis silvestris lybica

Description A slender animal resembling a grey house cat. The colour varies from grey to dark grey, with reddish to dusky red stripes on the legs and tail. The forehead is slightly darker while the throat and chest are lighter in colour, with a reddish tinge. The back of the ears also have a reddish tinge. African Wild Cats are larger than Small Spotted Cats and have more spots. They easily interbreed with domestic cats, but these cross-breeds have shorter legs and lack the reddish tinge on the back of the ears.

Sexual dimorphism Females have a lighter build than males.

Habitat African Wild Cats are found everywhere, provided there is sufficient dense thickets, tall grass and rocks for shelter.

Habits These shy, cunning animals are usually solitary, except during the mating season when one or more males are with a female. They are mainly nocturnal but can sometimes be seen late in the afternoon at sunset. They are territorial and both sexes will defend their areas. Although they are mainly terrestrial (and often use the same footpaths), they are also good tree climbers, especially when they are being pursued. They sometimes hunt in trees.

Voice Growl, hiss and purr.

Breeding 2 to 5 young are born any time of the year (peaking during September to March), after a gestation period of ± 2 months.

Mass ♂ 1,5–1,7 kg.
♀ 1,0–1,4 kg.

Food Mainly mice and spiders but also reptiles, insects and birds.

Life expectancy Unknown.

Enemies Leopard, lion.

± 2,5 cm

Small Spotted Cat

Klein Gekolde Kat
Felis nigripes

Description This is the smallest cat in the region. The colour varies from cinnamon in the south to light yellow-brown in the north. The coat is marked with stripes and spots. There are four black stripes down the back of the neck, the outer two extending over the shoulders. The shorter stripes often break up into spots. There are three rings around the throat and the tail is short. The Small Spotted Cat is distinguished from the African Wild Cat by its smaller size, lighter colour, and the spots and stripes which are more distinct.

Sexual dimorphism Males are slightly heavier than females.

Habitat Dry areas with enough open space as well as tall grass and shrubs for shelter.

Habits Small Spotted Cats are very shy, nocturnal animals which only appear after dusk. They are very seldom seen during the day. They are usually solitary but are occasionally seen in pairs. They move and hunt on the ground, but are also good tree climbers. In wooded areas, like the Kalahari, they take to trees when alarmed. By day they sleep in old antbear or springhare holes, in hollow antheaps or under shrubs. They are very aggressive for their size and are not as easily tamed as other wild cats.

Voice Spit and growl.

Breeding 1 to 3 young are born from November to December after a gestation period of ± 2 months.

Also known as Black-footed Cat.

Mass ♂ 46–79 kg.
♀ 56–80 kg.

Food Any carrion, from fresh meat to skins and bones.

Life expectancy
± 25 years.

Enemies Lion, crocodile.

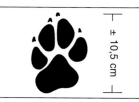

± 10,5 cm

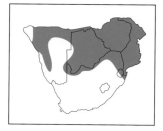

Spotted Hyaena

Gevlekte Hiëna
Crocuta crocuta

Description The Spotted Hyaena is a dull yellow to white, with irregular dark brown spots. The snout and the lower parts of the legs are dark brown. The young are dark brown to black. The animal has a large, broad head with round ears, a strong neck and forequarters, and a sloping back. The front paws are larger than the hind paws. The Spotted Hyaena is distinguished from the Brown Hyaena by its spots, round ears and shorter hair. The Aardwolf is smaller and has stripes instead of spots.

Sexual dimorphism Females are slightly larger than males.

Habitat Savannah, open plains and woodland where there is sufficient game.

Habits Spotted Hyaena are gregarious, forming groups in which the females are dominant. Groups are usually small (2 or 3), although up to 11 animals have been seen together. They frequently move about alone. Although mainly nocturnal, they are also seen in the early mornings or late afternoons. Their senses of smell, hearing and sight are acute. Spotted Hyaena are mainly scavengers but they also hunt in groups, chasing their prey until it is exhausted. As a group they sometimes try to drive lion and cheetah away from a kill.

Voice A very typical sound of the African night: the "whooo-hoop" which starts low and ends high. Otherwise they make loud, fearsome cries and high-pitched laughing sounds.

Breeding 1 to 4 young are born any time of the year (peaking in February to March), after a gestation period of ± 3½ months.

Also known as Laughing Hyaena.

Mass	♂ 35–57 kg.
	♀ 28–48 kg.

Food Mainly carrion, but also ground birds, reptiles and small mammals.

Life expectancy ± 24 years.

Enemies Lion, leopard.

± 8 cm

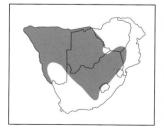

Brown Hyaena

Bruinhiëna
Parahyaena brunnea

Description The animal is a dark brown with a light yellow-brown "cloak" on the shoulders and neck. The forehead and belly are a dirty white colour. The legs have light brown rings. The hair is long and thick. The forequarters are more strongly developed than the hindquarters, the back sloping downwards. The head is large and the ears pointed. The Brown Hyaena differs from the lighter coloured Spotted Hyaena, in having longer hair, pointed ears and no spots. It is also much larger and darker in colour than the Aardwolf.

Sexual dimorphism Females are smaller than males.

Habitat Open, dry woodland or open shrubby areas with shrubs or tall grass patches for shelter.

Habits Brown Hyaena are gregarious and establish a territory, but some males are solitary. They usually forage alone over large areas. They are shy, mainly nocturnal animals but are also seen in the early mornings and late afternoons. During the day they rest under thick bushes or in holes. They are scavengers and, in contrast to Spotted Hyaenas, seldom hunt larger animals. They are strong diggers and dig their own shelters or make use of old antbear holes. The group has a communal dung heap.

Voice Yelp, squeal, snort and growl.

Breeding 2 to 5 young are born from August to November after a gestation period of ± 3 months.

Richard du Toit

Nigel Dennis

Mass 7,7–13,6 kg.

Food Termites, especially harvester termites, and other insects. No meat.

Life expectancy ± 13 years.

Enemies Leopard, lion.

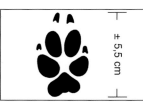

± 5,5 cm

Aardwolf

Aardwolf
Proteles cristatus

Description The colour of the body varies from yellow-brown to dull yellow, with approximately five distinct vertical black stripes on the flanks and some on the legs. It has a long, dark-tipped mane on the back which bristles when the animal is alarmed. The snout and lower parts of the legs are black. The ears stand erect and are pointed. The tail is bushy with a black tip. The Aardwolf is smaller than both hyaenas, with a lighter colour than the Brown Hyaena and lacking the spots of the Spotted Hyaena.

Sexual dimorphism None.

Habitat Dry open country, open patches around pans, grassy plains and dry vleis.

Habits Aardwolfs are usually solitary but pairs and family groups are also seen. They are nocturnal animals which sleep or hide in old antbear holes or holes which they dig themselves. They are neither carnivores nor scavengers and are sometimes wrongly identified as hyaenas. They have an acute sense of sight and of hearing. Their defence consists of using their long canine teeth, if necessary, or bristling their manes, which makes them appear much larger, especially in the dark. When alarmed they give a very loud roar for their size.

Voice A loud roar and a growl followed by a short bark.

Breeding 2 to 4 young are born from September to April after a gestation period of ± 2 months.

Mass 20–32 kg.

Food Only fresh meat, especially impala, springbok and also blue wildebeest.

Life expectancy ± 10 years.

Enemies Leopard, lion.

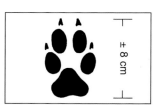

± 8 cm

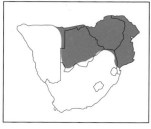

African Wild Dog

Wildehond
Lycaon pictus

Description These animals have a short dark snout, large round ears and fairly long hair. The long white tail which is raised when they are excited, is characteristic. The body and legs are white with yellow, brown and black blotches. The colour pattern differs among individuals. The hair between the eyes and ears is lighter with a dark stripe down the centre of the forehead and over the back of the head.

Sexual dimorphism None.

Habitat Open areas and plains in woodland.

Habits African Wild Dogs live in packs of about 10 to 15 animals with a male or female as leader. Larger packs of 40 or more animals have also been reported. They are mainly diurnal, and are active during the early mornings and late afternoons when they range over large areas in search of food. Spotted Hyaenas sometimes try to join the meal but usually get bullied. The young feed on food regurgitated by the adults.

Hunting habits The African Wild Dog is more dependent on its eyesight than on its sense of smell. These animals hunt in groups, chasing their prey until it is exhausted and is eventually torn apart while still on the hoof.

Voice Excited "barking chirping" noises, a barking growl or a "huu-huuu".

Breeding 7 to 10 young are born from March to July after a gestation period of ± 2½ months. (A litter of 19 has been recorded.)

Also known as Cape Hunting Dog or Wild Dog.

Dave Hamman/Gallo

Burger Cillié

Mass ♂ 7,3–12,0 kg. ♀ 7,3–10,0 kg.

Food Carrion, wild fruit, hares, moles, mice, lizards, birds and insects.

Life expectancy ± 11 years.

Enemies Leopard, lion.

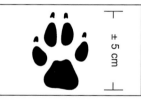

± 5 cm

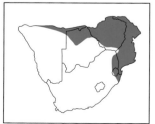

Side-striped Jackal

Witkwasjakkals
Canis adustus

Description The colour of this rather scarce jackal is grey or greyish-brown with a white stripe (sometimes a dark stripe) on the flanks. The snout is dark and the belly, throat and insides of the legs are a lighter colour, almost white. The tail is bushy and dark with a white tip. The ears stand erect, the tips being slightly rounded. It is distinguished from the Black-backed Jackal by the white tipped tail and by not having the black and white saddle.

Sexual dimorphism Females are slightly smaller than males.

Habitat They prefer well-watered terrain and avoid arid areas, open grasslands and mountainous areas.

Habits Side-striped Jackals are shy and seldom seen. They usually forage alone, but pairs and females with their young may be seen. Although they are mainly nocturnal they are also active at twilight. During the day they rest in old antbear holes or other shelters. When moving they walk or trot slowly. They are scavengers, but may hunt small animals.

Voice A series of pitiful yelps.

Breeding 2 to 6 young are born from August to January after a gestation period of 2 to 2½ months.

Mass	♂ 6,8–11,4 kg.
	♀ 5,5–10,0 kg.

Food Carrion, small mammals, lambs, birds, insects and wild fruit.

Life expectancy
± 13 years.

Enemies Leopard, lion.

± 6,5 cm

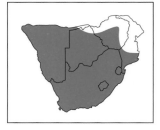

Black-backed Jackal

Rooijakkals
Canis mesomelas

Description The body and legs are a light reddish-brown to orange-brown. The throat, underparts and insides of the legs are whitish. The most outstanding feature is the black saddle on the back which is broad on the shoulders and narrow towards the bushy, black tail. The ears stand erect and are more pointed at the tips than those of the Side-striped Jackal. The latter animal lacks the black saddle, whereas the Black-backed Jackal lacks the white stripes on the flanks and the white tip to the tail.

Sexual dimorphism Males are slightly larger than females.

Habitat They occur in most habitats, even in the most arid areas. They avoid well-watered areas.

Habits Black-backed Jackal generally hunt and feed alone but actually live in pairs, establishing a territory for themselves. They are diurnal and nocturnal and are usually seen towards sunrise or sunset and in the early hours of the night. These cunning, shy animals have an acute sense of smell. They usually move at a quick trot. They are scavengers, as well as hunters of small animals and birds, and are able to go without water for long periods. During the day they rest in old antbear holes or other shelters. Black-backed Jackal still occur outside conservation areas and are more common than Side-striped Jackal.

Voice A long, frightening "njaaa" and a "na-ha-ha-ha" sound.

Breeding 1 to 6 (exceptionally 9) young are born from July to October after a gestation period of ± 2 months.

Veronica Roodt

Niel Cillié

Mass ♂ 3,4–4,9 kg.
♀ 3,2–5,3 kg.

Food Insects such as locusts, harvester termites and larvae, scorpions.

Life expectancy ± 12 years.

Enemies Brown hyaena, leopard, lion.

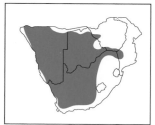

Bat-eared Fox

Bakoorvos
Otocyon megalotis

Description The colouring is a light brownish-grey with a lighter belly. The throat and forehead are also a lighter brown-grey. The margins of the ears and the legs are black. The handsome coat is fluffy. The bushy black tail, ending in a black tip, and the large ears are characteristic. As it is not a jackal it is correctly named the Bat-eared Fox and is distinguished from the Cape Fox by its larger ears and the absence of the Cape Fox's silvery sheen.

Sexual dimorphism Females are slightly heavier than males.

Habitat Open areas in dry savannah or semi-arid areas.

Habits Bat-eared Foxes are found either in pairs or in family groups of up to six members. They are both diurnal and nocturnal. During the heat of the day they rest in cool places such as old antbear holes or holes which they dig. Their senses of hearing and smell are very keen, enabling them for example, to find insect larvae underground. Contrary to popu-lar belief, they do not prey on sheep or lambs.

Voice A "who-who" sound, or a shrill, chattering alarm call by the young.

Breeding 2 to 6 young are born from September to November after a gestation period of ± 2 months.

Mass ♂ ± 2,8 kg.
♀ ± 2,5 kg.

Food Insects and reptiles as well as smaller mammals (mice), spiders and birds.

Life expectancy Unknown.

Enemies Leopard, lion, python.

± 4 cm

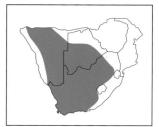

Cape Fox

Silwervos
Vulpes chama

Description The coat appears to be silvery-grey at close range, but grey at a distance. The upper front legs are reddish-brown and there are dark brown patches on the buttocks. The head is reddish-brown and the cheeks white, the throat is dull yellow and the belly white with a ruddy sheen. The tail is darker in colour, and long and bushy with a black tip. It is the only true fox in Southern Africa. It is more slender than the Bat-eared Fox and the ears are not as large.

Sexual dimorphism Males are slightly heavier than females.

Habitat Open plains with or without shrubs, open dry areas with trees, Karoo bushveld and fynbos.

Habits The Cape Fox is solitary and mainly nocturnal. It is most active just after sunset and just before sunrise. During the day it sleeps in a hole in the ground or in the shelter of tall grass. It defends a small area around its den when raising young. The Cape Fox is a strong digger and digs its own burrow or simply adapts an old springhare hole. It is a skilled mice hunter but, contrary to popular belief, does not prey on sheep or lambs.

Voice A high-pitched, howling bark.

Breeding 1 to 5 young are born from October to November after a gestation period of ± 2 months.

Koos Delport

Niel Cillié

Mass 7,9–14,5 kg.

Food Honey and young bees, birds, fruit, scorpions, spiders and reptiles.

Life expectancy ± 24 years.

Enemies Lion, python.

± 8 cm

Honey Badger

Ratel
Mellivora capensis

Description The body is black with a broad white, or brownish to greyish-white, saddle on the head and back. It is a stocky animal with short legs, equipped with strong claws which are ideal for digging. The hindquarters appear to be higher than the shoulders. The tail is short and black, and the ears small. The skin is very thick and loose, protecting it from attacks by predators.

Sexual dimorphism None.

Habitat They are very adaptable and occur in most types of habitat, except mountainous forests and deserts.

Habits Honey Badgers are usually solitary, but groups of two or three have been seen. Although they are mainly nocturnal, they are often seen during daytime. They usually rest during the heat of day. The walk is a rolling gait with the nose held close to the ground. With their claws they dig out spiders, scorpions, reptiles and bees. It is said that the Greater Honeyguide bird leads the Honey Badger to a beehive, waits until it has opened the hive and then joins in the feeding. Honey badgers are courageous and can be very aggressive, often fighting other animals. Like the Striped Polecat, they give off a sharp, unpleasant odour when alarmed.

Voice Growl, grunt, a high-pitched bark and a nasal "harrr-harrr".

Breeding Usually two young are born from October to January after a gestation period of ± 6 months.

Also known as Ratel.

Aaron Frankental/Gallo

Anthony Bannister/Gallo

Mass ♂ 9,5–13,2 kg.
♀ 9,7–20,0 kg.

Food Insects, mice, wild fruit, reptiles, frogs and birds.

Life expectancy ± 12 years.

Enemies Lion, leopard, python.

± 6 cm

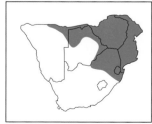

African Civet

Siwet
Civettictis civetta

Description This cat-like animal is a whitish-grey with indistinct spots on the forequarters and regular black spots which merge into stripes on the hindquarters. The black stripe down the back starts between the ears and extends to the base of the tail. The African Civet has a collar of white hair framed with black. The legs are black; the tail white, bushy and ringed, with a black tip. The face is black with two white patches on either side of the nose; the ears are rounded with white tips.

Sexual dimorphism Males have a slighter build than females.

Habitat Woodlands with thick undergrowth. They prefer well-watered surroundings.

Habits African Civet are exclusively nocturnal and are most active during the early evening or just before sunrise, when they can sometimes be seen. They are mainly solitary. They can climb trees but mostly move on the ground, usually using footpaths and walking purposefully with their heads held down. They are very shy and when disturbed stand motionless or lie down on the ground, depending on good camouflage rather than flight.

Voice A low, threatening growl and a coughing bark. They scream when fighting.

Breeding 1 to 4 young are born from August to December after a gestation period of ± 2 months.

Nigel Dennis

Reg Gush

Mass ♂ 1,6–2,6 kg.
♀ 1,5–2,3 kg.

Food Mice, rats, grasshoppers, beetles, spiders, birds, snakes.

Life expectancy ± 12 years.

Enemies Lion, leopard, python.

± 3 cm

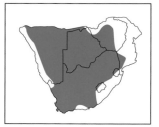

Small-spotted Genet

Kleinkolmuskejaatkat
Genetta genetta

Description: A cat-like animal with a long slender body and short legs. The tail is also very long with black and white rings. The large ears are thin and rounded. The colour of the body is greyish-white with black to rusty-brown spots. The dark crest of hair is longer than that of the Large-spotted Genet, its chin is darker and the tail ends in a white tip. The spots of the Large-spotted Genet are larger, its chin is white and the tail ends in a black tip.

Sexual dimorphism: None

Habitat: Prefers more arid and more open areas than the Large-spotted Genet. Woodland with dry marshes or grassplains; also arid shrubveld and dry riverine forest.

Habits: Predominantly nocturnal and rests during the day in shelters such as holes in the ground or holes in treetrunks. Usually solitary or in pairs. Forages on the ground but can take to trees after prey or when chased. Moves with a fast trot in a low stalking position, with its tail horizontal behind it. When stalking prey it moves very slowly into a suitable position to attack.

Voice Growls and spits.

Breeding 2 to 4 young are born from August to September after a gestation period of 10 to 11 weeks.

Mass 1,4–3,2 kg.

Food Rats, mice, locusts, beetles, birds, spiders, crickets, frogs and crabs.

Life expectancy ± 13 years.

Enemies Leopard, lion, python.

± 3 cm

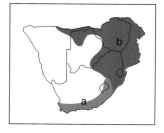

Large-spotted Genet

Grootkolmuskejaatkat
Genetta tigrina

Rusty-spotted Genet

Rooikolmuskejaatkat
Genetta maculata

Description These rather small, cat-like animals are white or greyish-white with dark spots and stripes. The tail is long and dark with white rings. This species has now been split into the **Large-spotted Genet** *Genetta tigrina* (top & a) with black spots, stripes and rings, and the **Rusty-spotted Genet** *Genetta maculata* (bottom & b) with rust-brown stripes and spots. A distinct band of dark hair extends from just behind the shoulders to the base of the tail. There are white spots below the eyes and the cheeks are white. These two white areas are divided by dark brown stripes extending from the corners of the eyes. The rounded ears stand erect. Distinguished from the Small-spotted Genet by the dark tip of the tail and the white chin.

Sexual dimorphism None.

Habitat Well-watered areas with sufficient under-growth.

Habits Usually solitary but pairs are sometimes found. They are nocturnal, only emerging a few hours after sunset. During the day they sleep in old Aardvark or Springhare holes or in hollow tree stumps. They are mainly terrestrial but sometimes take shelter or hunt in trees. Their movements are watchful and furtive, and when they run they hold their heads down and their tails horizontal.

Voice Growl and spit.

Breeding 2 to 5 young are born from August to March after a gestation period of ± 2 months.

Genetta tigrina

Genetta maculata

Mass ♂ 681–1 460 g.
♀ 596–880 g.

Food Insects and mice, but also reptiles, spiders, scorpions and millipedes.

Life expectancy
± 8 years.

Enemies Brown hyaena, black-backed jackal.

± 3 cm

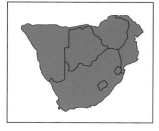

Striped Polecat

Stinkmuishond
Ictonyx striatus

Description A small predator with short legs. The colour is black with four white stripes originating in a white patch on the head, extending almost parallel along the back and flanks, to meet again at the base of the tail. There are white patches below the ears as well as on the forehead. The tail is thick and woolly with long black and white hair. This animal differs from the African Striped Weasel which has a smaller, elongated body and lacks the white patches below the ears.

Sexual dimorphism Males are larger than females.

Habitat Found in all types of habitat – from desert-like areas with shrubs to forests, but nowhere common.

Habits Mainly solitary but pairs or females with their young have been seen. They are territorial, nocturnal animals, becoming active late at night and are very seldom seen during the day. They usually run with their backs humped. They make use of the old holes of other animals or take shelter under rock piles or in rock clefts, but sometimes dig their own holes if the soil is soft. The nauseous exudation from the anal glands is used as a last resort in self-defence.

Voice Growl and bark.

Breeding 1 to 3 young are born from October to March after a gestation period of 5 to 6 weeks.

Mass 440–900 g.

Food Beetles, termites, crickets, locusts, mice, ground birds and reptiles.

Life expectancy ± 12 years.

Enemies Leopard, lion, brown hyaena, African wild cat, black-backed jackal.

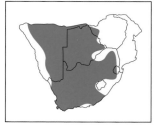

Yellow Mongoose

Witkwasmuishond
Cynictus penicillata

Description Over most of its range the colour varies from yellowish-red in the south-east through shades of yellow to greyish-yellow in the north-west, with a white tip on the tail. In the northern parts of Botswana the animals are grey with speckles without the white tip to the tail. They are also much smaller with shorter hair and tails. The legs, chin, chest and throat of the Yellow Mongoose are slightly lighter in colour than the rest of the body. The Slender Mongoose is sometimes also yellowish, but always has a black-tipped tail.

Sexual dimorphism None.

Habitat Open grassy plains. They usually avoid bushy areas.

Habits They are gregarious animals and are found in colonies of 20 and more. The colonies in Botswana are usually smaller. Yellow Mongooses often live socially with Ground Squirrels and Meerkats but may also dig their own burrows. These consist of many tunnels, corridors and entrances. The animals are mainly diurnal but are sometimes active after dusk. They forage far away from their dwelling holes and, when danger threatens, they make use of any shelter available.

Voice Unknown.

Breeding 2 to 5 young are born from October to March after a gestation period of ± 8 weeks.

Mass ♂ 450–640 g.	
♀ 410–530 g.	

Food Termites, beetles, locusts, ants, lizards, fruit, mice, bird eggs.

Life expectancy ± 8 years.

Enemies Leopard, lion, black-backed jackal, civet.

Slender Mongoose

Swartkwasmuishond
Galerella sanguinea

Kaokoland Slender Mongoose

Kaokolandse Swartkwasmuishond
Galerella flavescens

Description This slender built mongoose has a long tail with a black tip (hence its Afrikaans name). When its moves, the tail is characteristically bent in a bow, similar to that of a lion. This species is now divided into the **Slender Mongoose** *Galerella sanguinea* (top & a) with a speckled brown to reddish brown colour, and the **Kaokoland Slender Mongoose** *Galerella flavescens*, (bottom & b) with a speckled dark reddish brown colour and the last third of the tail black. (The latter is a former subspecies *G. s. nigrata* occurring in Namibia.) The Yellow Mongoose is usually more yellowish with a white-tipped tail.

Sexual dimorphism Males are slightly larger than females.

Habitat A typical savannah species. Also occurs in more open areas, provided there is sufficient shelter such as rocks, termite heaps and old tree trunks.

Habits Are mainly diurnal and appear a while after sunrise. They forage solitarily. Are mainly terrestrial but sometimes climb trees to hunt or evade enemies. When frightened they usually freeze in their tracks or stand on their hindfeet to observe their surroundings. They move with a fast gait and prefer footpaths. Often seen hastily crossing a road.

Voice Silent, young "hey-nwee".

Breeding 1 to 2 young born from October to March.

± 3 cm

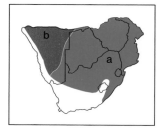

Galerella sanguinea

Clem Haagner

Galerella flavescens

Niel Cillié

Mass ♂ 680–1 250 g.
♀ 490–900 g.

Food Insects, mice, carrion, birds and reptiles.

Life expectancy Unknown.

Enemies Leopard, caracal, black-backed jackal.

± 3,5 cm

Cape Grey Mongoose

Kleingrysmuishond
Galerella pulverolenta

Description Belongs to the same genus and is replaced by the Slender Mongoose to the north. From a distance it looks grey, but from closer it is actually black with white or yellowish-brown speckles. Animals from the north-west are more brown than the paler ones of the south. The hair on the head is short and lies flat, the ears slightly covered. The hair at the base of the tail is long and becomes shorter towards the tip. The underparts are without the speckles and the legs are darker than the upper parts.

Sexual dimorphism Males are slightly larger than females.

Habitat Utilises a variety of habitats; from fynbos and forests to very dry or mountainous areas, even parts with sparse vegetation.

Habits Diurnal with a decrease of activity during the warmer time of day. Usually solitary, sometimes in pairs. Young stay in the breeding burrows till weaned, then start moving around independently. They are mainly terrestrial, but can hunt in trees. Uses stacks of rocks, holes in termite heaps, as well as other holes for shelter, if sufficient vegetation is not available. Are not afraid of humans and prefer walking in footpaths.

Voice Unknown.

Breeding Young are usually born from August to December.

Also known as Small Grey Mongoose.

| Mass | ♂ ± 4,5 kg. |
| | ♀ ± 4,1 kg. |

Food Beetles, termites, locusts, mice, frogs, ground birds, snakes, fruit

Life expectancy Unknown

Enemies Leopard, lion.

± 5,5 cm

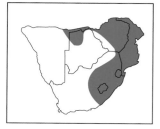

White-tailed Mongoose

Witstertmuishond
Ichneumia albicauda

Description A very large grey-brown mongoose with relatively long black legs. The last four-fifths of the long tail are covered with long white hair (hence its name). The head is a slightly lighter colour than the rest of the body. The long hind legs cause its back to slant forward when it walks. Meller's Mongoose (sometimes also with a white tail) is smaller and more brown. Selous Mongoose is smaller.

Sexual dimorphism Males are slightly heavier than females.

Habitat Woodlands with plentiful water. Also along rivers and marshes in drier regions, but prefers moist savannahs.

Habits They are nocturnal animals, emerging only shortly after dark. They are usually only active for the first part of night. They are terrestrial and sleep during the day in old Aardvark or Springhare holes, or in a thick bush. Jog with their noses close to the ground. When alarmed, the crest of long hair on the back rises. They are often close to human activities, where they hunt chickens and other domestic animals.

Voice Mostly silent; growl, bark.

Breeding 1 to 3 young are born from September to December.

Luke Hunter/Gallo

Lex Hes

Mass 2,4–4,1 kg.

Food Frogs, spur-toed frogs, crabs, mice, swamp rats, fish and insects.

Life expectancy ± 11 years.

Enemies Lion, serval, python, African hawk eagle.

± 6 cm

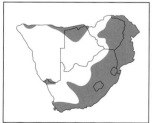

Marsh Mongoose

Watermuishond
Atilax paludinosus

Description A rather large mongoose. The colour of the body varies from almost black to rust-brown and is sometimes speckled. The colour of the underparts, the head and the face is the same as the rest of the body, while the legs are darker and the chin and cheeks may be lighter. The hair is long, especially on the tail. The head is large and broad and the small ears lie flat. The Marsh Mongoose differs from the White-tailed Mongoose which is larger, darker in colour and has a white tail.

Sexual dimorphism None.

Habitat Always near rivers, streams, marshes, swamps, dams and estuaries.

Habits A solitary animal except when the female has young, which then follow her. It is active from dawn till mid-morning and again in the late afternoon till dusk. It is active for a longer period on overcast days, sleeps in thick shelter and prefers footpaths or the muddy banks of streams or dams when foraging. It is an excellent swimmer, sometimes taking to water when alarmed.

Voice Growl and a high-pitched, explosive bark.

Breeding 1 to 3 young are born from August to December.

Also known as Water Mongoose.

Mass 1,0–1,6 kg.

Food Insects, snails, reptiles, worms, bird eggs, fruit and locusts.

Life expectancy ± 8 years.

Enemies Leopard, lion, black-backed jackal, civet, python, African hawk eagle.

± 3 cm

cm 1 2 3 4 5 6 7 8 9 10

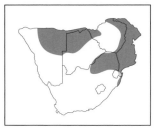

Banded Mongoose

Gebande Muishond
Mungos mungo

Description A small mongoose with colour varying from light grey to reddish-brown with speckles. The colour of the limbs is the same as the rest of the body. Dark crossbands, which are characteristic, start in the centre of the back and end on the crop. The dark, reddish-brown Eastern species has black bands and a black tail tip, while those of the Western species are brown. The animal has small, round ears and a pointed snout.

Sexual dimorphism None.

Habitat Riverine forest and dense *Acacia* woodland with sufficient undergrowth, antheaps, fallen logs and other dry plant material.

Habits Banded Mongooses are gregarious animals which live in colonies of 30 or more. They forage individually but keep contact by means of a continuous twittering. When in danger, or on hearing an alarm call, they all keep quiet, while some stand on their hind legs to keep watch on their surroundings. They will then either continue to feed or quietly run away and seek temporary shelter in holes. They are diurnal, sleeping in holes in hollow antheaps or antbear holes. They can climb trees but usually move on the ground.

Voice Twittering. The alarm call is a loud chattering noise.

Breeding 2 to 8 young are born from October to February after a gestation period of ± 8 weeks.

Mass 210–340 g.

Food Termites, insects, worms, snails, scorpions, locusts, reptiles, earthworms.

Life expectancy ± 6 years.

Enemies Leopard, lion, civet, African wild cat, black-backed jackal, python.

± 2,5 cm

Dwarf Mongoose

Dwergmuishond
Helogale parvula

Description This is the smallest of all the mongooses in the region. From a distance it appears to be dark brown but on closer inspection the colour is dark brown to rust-brown with fine, light-coloured speckles. The hair is sparser underneath the belly but of the same colour. Although the ears are small, they are more prominent than those of the other mongooses owing to the very short hair on the head. The claws on the front feet are long and well developed for digging.

Sexual dimorphism None.

Habitat In dry woodland with hard, stony ground and where there are anthills, fallen logs and other detritus.

Habits Dwarf Mongooses are gregarious animals living in colonies of 10 or more. Such a colony inhabits a permanent shelter which is either an old anthill or a hole dug by themselves, with the entrance usually under an old log. They are diurnal, appearing only long after sunrise and returning again before sunset. They are terrestrial and feed far apart but keep contact by means of "chook" noises. When the alarm call is given, they all stiffen – some will stand on their hind legs to search for the source of danger. They are fond of lying in the sun.

Voice "Perrip" or "chook", or "shu-shwe" for the alarm call.

Breeding 2 to 4 young are born from October to March after a gestation period of ± 8 weeks.

Mass 620–960 g.

Food Worms, insects, larvae, mice, millipedes, spiders and scorpions.

Life expectancy ± 12 years.

Enemies Leopard, lion, black-backed jackal, brown hyaena.

± 3,5 cm

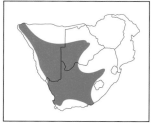

Meerkat

Stokstertmeerkat
Suricata suricatta

Description The colour is silvery-brown, sometimes slightly paler. Darker spots, which become more obvious from the shoulders towards the rump and sometimes form crosslines, can be seen on the back. The dark tipped tail is characteristic. The animal has a broad head, a short snout which ends in a sharp tip, and a dark area around the eyes. The fine, dark stripe above the eyes extends to the top of the ears. The hindquarters are more heavily built than the forequarters.

Sexual dimorphism None.

Habitat Open areas on hard calcareous or stony soil.

Habits Meerkat are playful, diurnal animals. They only emerge from their holes after sunrise, where they usually sit for quite a while with their bellies turned towards the sun. They live in colonies of up to 20 animals and use old burrows of Ground Squirrels, or dig their own with many tunnels, corridors and entrances. A typical posture is standing on the hind legs, or sitting upright to watch the surroundings. When not playing, they are usually busy digging or turning over stones in search of food.

Voice The alarm call is a sharp, loud bark.

Breeding 2 to 5 young are born from October to March after a gestation period of 10 to 11 weeks.

Also known as Suricate.

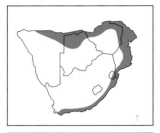

Large Grey Mongoose

Grootgrysmuishond
Herpestes ichneumon

Description The colour is grey, the hair long and coarse, and the legs are short turning black towards the feet. It has an elongated head and body.

Habitat River edges, dams and marshes.

Habits Diurnal and nocturnal; they rest in reed beds or under bushes. They forage in pairs or small groups. When under stress, they raise their fur.

Breeding Two young are born in early summer.

Length ± 100 cm.	
Mass ♂ ± 3,4 kg.	
♀ ± 3,1 kg.	

Food Mice, birds, reptiles, frogs and insects.

Life expectancy
Unknown

Enemies Leopard, lion, python, large raptors.

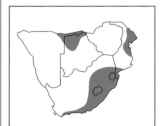

Spotted-necked Otter

Kleinotter
Lutra maculicolis

Description It has an elongated body, slim build and a broad head. The colour is brown with white blotches on the chest and throat.

Habitat Close to permanent rivers and marshes.

Habits More aquatic than the African Clawless Otter. Only leaves the water to rest or excrete; is clumsy on land. Usually solitary and active at twilight.

Breeding 2 to 3 young are born in summer.

Length ± 100 cm.	
Mass ♂ ± 4,5 kg.	
♀ ± 3,5 kg.	

Food Fish, crabs, molluscs, frogs and birds.

Life expectancy
Unknown

Enemies Python.

Herpestes ichneumon

Clem Haagner

Lutra maculicolis

Roger de la Harpe

Mass 10–18 kg.

Food Mainly frogs and crabs, but also fish, birds, insects and reptiles.

Life expectancy ± 15 years.

Enemy Python.

± 12,5 cm

African Clawless Otter

Groototter
Aonyx capensis

Description The coat, which is valuable as fur, consists of a dense covering of shiny protective hair. The upper parts of the body are brown, the rest being slightly lighter in colour. The hindquarters are usually darker than the forequarters. The throat and sides of the face are white up to the ears and eyes. The toes of the hind feet are distinctly webbed. African Clawless Otters can be distinguished from Spotted-necked Otters by their larger size, by the unspotted white area on the chest and throat reaching up to below the ears and eyes, and by the lack of claws on the forefeet.

Sexual dimorphism None.

Habitat Usually in or near rivers, well-watered marshes, dams or lakes, but they sometimes wander far from water in search of new feeding grounds.

Habits Usually solitary, but pairs and family groups are also seen. Mainly diurnal, they are usually active in the early morning and late afternoon but sometimes during the night as well. When it is hot, they rest in dry shelters among rocks or reeds but most of the day is spent in the water. Upon emerging they shake their heads and then their bodies, and slide onto the bank to dry themselves. They are very playful animals, chasing each other in the water.

Voice A high-pitched scream, a contented purring growl, also hisses and growls when angry. The alarm call is an explosive "ha".

Breeding 1, seldom 2, young are born any time of the year after a gestation period of ± 9 weeks.

Also known as Cape Clawless Otter.

Top – Tree Squirrel (Burger Cillié). Right – South African Galago (Clem Haagner/Gallo)

Small Mammals

All the other

small browsers,

omnivores and

insectivores.

Mass	♂ 41–65 kg.
	♀ 40–58 kg.

Food Mainly termites, sometimes even ants.

Life expectancy ± 10 years.

Enemies Leopard, lion, brown hyaena.

± 11 cm

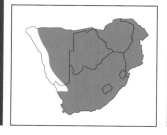

Aardvark

Erdvark
Orycteropus afer

Description This animal has long ears, a long pig-like snout and a thick tail. The skin is almost bare and of a yellow-grey colour while the hair on the legs is darker in colour. It also takes on the colour of the soil of its habitat. The hindquarters are much heavier than the forequarters, with the shoulders lower than the crop. The limbs are powerful and the feet, especially the forefeet, are equipped with strong claws adapted for digging and for breaking up anthills.

Sexual dimorphism Males are slightly more heavily built than females.

Habitat Aardvarks are very adaptable and occur where the soil is not very compact and where there are sufficient termites.

Habits Generally solitary, they range widely seeking food, with their noses held close to the ground. They are mainly nocturnal, usually sleeping in a hole which they fill in behind them. They can dig at an unbelievable rate. Three kinds of holes can be distinguished: the first hole in which they live and in which the young are born; secondly, a temporary shelter; and thirdly, a small excavation for the purpose of searching for food. Their teeth are poorly developed and they use their sticky tongues to catch termites.

Voice Snuffle and grunt.

Breeding A single young is born from July to September after a gestation period of ± 7 months.

Also known as Antbear.

Keith Begg/Gallo

Clem Haagner

Mass 4,5–14,5 kg.

Food Mainly ants and sometimes termites.

Life expectancy ± 12 years.

Enemies None.

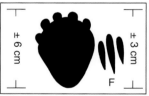

± 6 cm ± 3 cm F

Ground Pangolin

Ietermagog
Manis temminckii

Description The very hard, dark grey-brown scales, which cover the body like roof tiles, are characteristic. The animal has a small head and pointed snout, and the sides of the face are devoid of scales. It walks on its hind legs with the forelegs held off the ground, only touching it now and then. The forefeet are equipped with long, curved claws with which it digs. It is an odd animal and is very seldom seen.

Sexual dimorphism None.

Habitat Sandy soil in dry to fairly humid types of savannah with adequate shelter.

Habits Ground Pangolins are usually solitary and move about noisily as they brush against bushes and branches. They are mainly nocturnal but are sometimes seen during the day. If they suspect any intrusion, they stand upright on their hind legs, supported by their tails. They live in old antbear holes and hunt for food at night. When threatened they roll themselves into a ball. They can emit a bad odour when alarmed.

Voice An audible snuffling when feeding and a hiss when rolling up into a ball.

Breeding A single young is born from May to July after a gestation period of ± 4½ months.

Also known as Pangolin.

Koos Delport

Ulrich Oberprieler

Mass ♀ 3,2–4,7 kg.
　　　♂ 2,5–4,2 kg.

Food Grass, shrubs and herbs.

Life expectancy ± 6 years.

Enemies Brown hyaena, leopard, lion, caracal, python, African hawk eagle, martial eagle, black eagle.

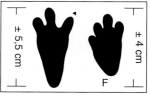

Rock Hyrax

Klipdassie
Procavia capensis

Description This is a small, stockily built, tailless animal. Its colour varies from grey-brown to ash-brown with a yellow or red tinge and fine black speckles. On the back is an oblong patch of black hair, which in other species is white or yellow. The hair around the mouth, behind the ears, above the eyes and on the underparts is lighter in colour. The Yellow-spotted Rock Hyrax's dorsal patch is yellow and it has white eyebrows. The Tree Hyrax differs from both as its hair is longer and more woolly.

Sexual dimorphism Males are slightly larger than females.

Habitat Rocks, cliffs and stony hills with a covering of bushes, and trees.

Habits Rock Hyraxes are hierarchical and live in colonies that may number from four to a few hundred. These mainly diurnal animals prefer to forage in the early morning and late afternoon, and even after dusk when there is sufficient moonlight. On cold days they sit in the morning sun to warm themselves before they begin to feed. Rock Hyraxes are good tree climbers. Few fights occur, but, when aggressive, they growl and show their teeth and the black hair on their back bristles.

Voice A sharp alarm bark. They also growl, snort, scream and chirp.

Breeding 1 to 6 young are born from September to October after a gestation period of ± 7½ months in the winter rainfall region and during March to April in the summer rainfall region.

Also known as Rock Dassie.

Mass ♂ 3,5–5,2 kg.
♀ 3,4–3,8 kg.

Food Roots, sprouts and stems of grass and reeds.

Life expectancy Unknown.

Enemies Serval, python.

± 8 cm

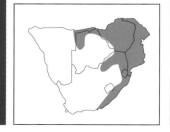

Greater Canerat

Grootrietrot
Thryonomys swinderianus

Description The largest of the two canerats in our region. A stockily built rodent with coarse, bristly hair and a relatively short tail. The general colour is brown with dark speckles, the underparts are lighter greyish-brown, with a white chin and throat. The ears are covered with hair. The elongated snout and nose forms a fleshy cushion, which is used in bump fights. The Lesser Canerat is smaller and occurs only in certain parts of Zimbabwe.

Sexual dimorphism Males are bigger than females.

Habitat Reedbeds and areas with long grass close to permanent rivers and marshes.

Habits These animals are not rats. They live in groups of 8 to 10 but forage alone. They are mainly nocturnal but also active at dawn to a certain extent. They rest during the day beneath thick vegetation or in holes in riverbanks. When chased, they run a distance, and then stop and listen to find out if they are still being pursued. They are good swimmers and sometimes take to the water when scared.

Voice Snort; a low whistle when alarmed.

Breeding 4 to 8 young are born from August to December after a gestation period of 4 to 5 months.

Mass 236–480 g.

Food Beetles, termites, millipedes, locusts, moths, earthworms, bird chicks.

Life expectancy ± 3 years

Enemies Lion, leopard, caracal.

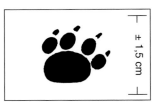

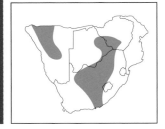

South African Hedgehog

Krimpvarkie
Atelerix frontalis

Description The body is covered with small short spines from the forehead, behind the ears, across the back and down the flanks. The spines are ringed with black and white or dull yellow, some being completely white. The legs are tall and covered with grey-brown hair. The face is framed with white hair across the forehead above the eyes and below the ears. The rest of the face is dark brown or black. The snout is pointed.

Sexual dimorphism None.

Habitat Found in a variety of habitats where sufficient food and dry shelter are available.

Habits Hedgehogs are mainly nocturnal but are sometimes seen in daytime after rain. During the day they rest curled up like a ball under thick layers of leaves, dense grass or bushes, or in holes. The resting place changes daily. The only semi-permanent resting place is where females keep their young, until they are able to move with her. Although hedgehogs have poor eyesight, they have a keen sense of smell. They can even locate food below the soil surface, which they then dig out. During the winter they become torpid, rarely emerging from their resting place.

Voice Snuffle, snort and growl or a high-pitched alarm call.

Breeding 1 to 9 young are born from October to April after a gestation period of ± 5 weeks.

Mass ♂ 10–19 kg. ♀ 10–24 kg.

Food Bulbs, tubers, roots, which they dig out; also vegetables, fruit and carrion.

Life expectancy ± 20 years.

Enemies Cheetah, leopard, lion, caracal.

± 8 cm

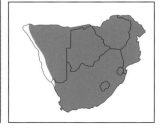

Cape Porcupine

Ystervark
Hystrix africaeaustralis

Description The largest rodent in the region. The body is covered with quills, spines and flattened, black bristles. The quills are white with black rings and are about 30 cm long. On the neck and back the quills and spines are longer and thinner and can be raised, which makes the animal look larger and more fearsome. The rest of the body, the face and the short legs are covered with coarse, black hair.

Sexual dimorphism Females are usually larger than males.

Habitat They are very adaptable and are found in most types of habitat except in forests and deserts.

Habits Cape Porcupines are usually solitary, but three or more adults may make use of the same shelter. One often sees old bones lying outside their burrows, which they dragged there. Sometimes they move long distances at night in search of food. They can run fast when chased. They cause much damage to agricultural lands and vegetable gardens. Quills are not released, as is commonly believed, but the animal backs up to the attacker so that the quills stick into and remain in the attacker. Sometimes lions and leopards have trouble after an attack when broken-off quills cause festering sores.

Voice Growl, snuffle, teeth-chattering; rattling their tail quills when alarmed.

Breeding 1 to 3 young are born any time of the year (peaking in August to March in summer rainfall areas), after a gestation period of ± 3 months.

Also known as Porcupine.

Anthony Bannister/Gallo

Anthony Bannister/Gallo

Mass ♂ 1,4–3,8 kg.
♀ 1,6–4,5 kg.

Food Grass, as well as leaves, rhizomes and stems.

Life expectancy
± 7 years.

Enemies Leopard, caracal, lion, African wild cat, African wild dog, martial eagle.

± 3,5 cm

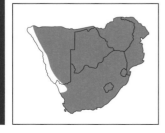

Scrub Hare

Kolhaas
Lepus saxatilis

Description It is the larger of the two hares. The colour is a dull yellow with blackish-grey speckles, giving a salt-and-pepper effect. The chin and stomach are white and the throat is ringed by a collar of the same colour as the upper parts. There is a white spot just above the eyes, and a patch on the nape of the neck which varies in colour from brick-red to orange-yellow. The tail is black on top and white underneath, and the feet are a dull yellow colour. The Scrub Hare is distinguished from the Cape Hare by its larger size and a preference for a more shrubby area.

Sexual dimorphism Females are slightly larger than males.

Habitat Thickets with patches of grasslands. They avoid open grass plains or dense bush.

Habits Scrub Hares are nocturnal, appearing only at sunset; at sunrise they return to their shelters. During cloudy weather they may graze in the mornings. They are sensitive to weather conditions; on cold evenings they are less active and in rainy weather they remain in their shelters. During the day they rest under bushes with their heads down and ears flat. They are usually solitary but also appear in pairs. They still occur outside conservation areas.

Voice Quiet animals, but they may scream loudly if handled.

Breeding 1 to 3 young are born any time of the year after a gestation period of ± 5 weeks.

Mass ♂ 1,4–1,8 kg.
   ♀ 1,5–2,3 kg.

Food Short grass. They do not drink water.

Life expectancy
± 5 years.

Enemies Leopard, caracal, lion, African wild cat, African wild dog, martial eagle.

± 3 cm

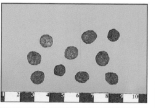

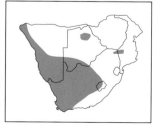

Cape Hare

Vlakhaas
Lepus capensis

Description The colour varies between two extremes. The hares from more humid regions are a dull yellow with blackish-grey speckles, the patch on the nape of the neck brown-pink and the tail black on top and white underneath. The hares from drier regions are grey-white, the patch on the nape of the neck light grey and the tail dull black above and white underneath. Around the eyes are fringes of light yellow hair, and just above the eyes are oblong, light brown spots. This animal differs from the Scrub Hare in that it is smaller and prefers more open areas.

Sexual dimorphism Females are slightly larger than males.

Habitat Open, dry grassy plains with patches of tall grass or shrubs for shelter.

Habits Cape Hares are solitary, nocturnal animals, which are seen only on cloudy days, or at sunrise and sunset. They are very sensitive to weather conditions. They are seldom seen on cold nights and remain in their shelters when it rains. During the day they rest in the shelter of tall grass or small bushes, lying down with their ears flat. In this position they lie motionless until danger is very close, before jumping up. They run remarkably fast, turning and swerving easily at high speed. They sometimes take shelter in old Aardvark or Springhare holes.

Voice Quiet animals, but make a soft grunt and can scream loudly when handled.

Breeding 1 to 3 young are born any time of the year (peaking in summer), after a gestation period of ± 6 weeks.

Peter Lillie/Gallo

Clem Haagner

Mass 1,3–3,1 kg.

Food Grass, especially young sprouts after veld fire.

Life expectancy
Unknown.

Enemies Leopard, caracal, African wild cat.

± 2,5 cm

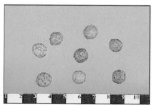

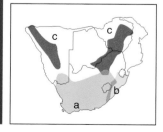

Red Rock Rabbits

Rooiklipkonyne
Pronolagus spp.

Differences between Hares and Rabbits Hares have longer hind feet than forefeet, which are less distinct in rabbits. Young of hares are independent early and are born with open eyes and with all their fur. Young of rabbits are born without fur and with closed eyes. The tail and feet of rock rabbits are more reddish-brown, while hares' tails are white with black on top.

Description Three red rock rabbits occur in our region, namely (a) **Smith's** (*P. rupestris*), (b) **Natal** (*P. crassicaudatus*) and (c) **Jameson's** (*P. randensis*) Red Rock Rabbit. The Natal Red Rock Rabbit is the largest and Smith's the smallest. The three species have very similar habitat requirements and habits and look very much alike. They have a thick, coarse, salt-and-pepper fur with a reddish brown colour, the underparts are rusty buff. All three species have whitish or whitish-grey chins and cheeks, but this colour extends on the Natal Red Rock Rabbit in a broad band along the lower jaw to meet with the lower edge of the hind neck spot.

Sexual dimorphism None.

Habitat Rocky areas like cliffs, stony hills with edible grass. They never move far away from their home range.

Habits Forages alone, but is usually part of a small group with communal manure heaps. During the day they sleep underneath rocks or in openings between rocks, sometimes in thick grass where they are not easily disturbed. They leave their shelters at sunset and forage through the night.

Voice Shrill scream if scared.

Breeding 1 or 2 young believed to be born in summer.

Pat Donaldson/Gallo

Burger Cillié

Mass 2,5–3,0 kg.

Food Grass, leaves, roots, rhizomes and corms.

Life expectancy ± 7 years.

Enemies Jackals, brown hyaena, spotted hyaena, cheetah, leopard, lion, caracal.

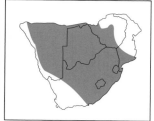

Springhare

Springhaas
Pedetes capensis

Description These rodents resemble kangaroos, the forelegs being short and the hind legs very long and powerful. The colour varies from a light fawnish-brown to yellow-brown. The long whiskers are black, the chin white and the lower parts off-white. The long tail is reddish and ends in a characteristic broad, black tip. The eyes are conspicuously large. Strong, curved claws on the forefeet are adapted to digging. The ears are narrow and erect.

Sexual dimorphism None.

Habitat Along rivers or pans with sediment and sandy silt soil. Also in sandveld. They avoid hard ground.

Habits Springhares are exclusively nocturnal, emerging from their burrows well after dark. The burrows, excavated on high ground to avoid flooding, branch out into passages, some having different entrances. A burrow is occupied by a single animal. They are accomplished diggers, loosening the soil with the forepaws and pushing it out with their powerful hind legs. They move with a hopping motion, using the hind legs only, all the while keeping the short forelegs held close to the body.

Voice Silent, but scream loudly when handled.

Breeding 1, exceptionally 2, young are born any time of the year after a gestation period of ± 10½ weeks.

Mass ♂ 511–1 022 g.
♀ 511–795 g.

Food Leaves, grass, stems bulbs, seeds, roots and sometimes insects.

Life expectancy
± 15 years.

Enemies Jackals, brown hyaena, leopard, lion, caracal, martial eagle.

± 7 cm   ± 3,5 cm

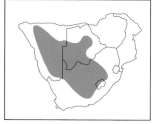

South African Ground Squirrel

Waaierstertgrondeekhoring
Xerus inaurus

Description The colour of the body is a light cinnamon with characteristic white stripes along the flanks. The lower parts of the legs, the belly, the sides of the neck and the areas around the eyes are white. The tail has long hair, is ringed with black and white, and has a white tip. When the animal stands on its hind legs the tail is spread like an open fan to give shade to its back and head. The ears are simple openings in the sides of the head. It is very difficult to distinguish between the Ground Squirrel and the Mountain Ground Squirrel in the field. The latter prefers a habitat on rocky hillsides, which is normally avoided by the Ground Squirrel.

Sexual dimorphism Males are slightly larger than females.

Habitat Open dry plains with hard calcareous soil and thinly spread bushes.

Habits Ground Squirrels are diurnal and live in colonies of up to 30 animals. They dig their own burrows about 80 cm underneath the ground, with many tunnels, corridors and entrances. Rooms in the burrows are lined with grass on which they rest. Such a burrow is occupied by a few females with their young. The dominant female will chase away all strangers from the immediate vicinity of the entrance. Males move from one group to another and stay only for a few weeks. The animals emerge from their burrows only after sunrise and return before sunset.

Voice A high-pitched whistle or scream for an alarm call, and an aggressive growl.

Breeding 1 to 3 young are born any time of the year after a gestation period of 6 to 7 weeks.

Mass ♂ 76–240 g,
♀ 108–265 g

Food Leaves, flowers, seeds, fruit, bark, berries and sometimes insects.

Life expectancy
± 8 years.

Enemies Leopard, lion, caracal, martial eagle.

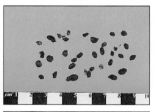

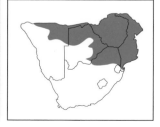

Tree Squirrel

Boomeekhoring
Paraxerus cepapi

Description The colour is variable – the upper parts vary from a speckled grey with a buffy tinge, to a speckled light colour. The flanks are always more yellowish and the underparts vary from white to buff. The limbs of the Southern race are yellowish without speckles. The tail is long and bushy and is indistinctly ringed with black. The Tree Squirrel differs from the Red Squirrel whose tail, belly and legs are more yellow or red than the body. The Striped Tree Squirrel is smaller and has white stripes on its flanks; the Sun Squirrel is larger and the tail, as a whole, is ringed with white.

Sexual dimorphism None.

Habitat A woodland species, living in mixed thornveld or mopani woodland.

Habits These animals forage alone but the Southern race live in groups consisting of one or two males, females and their young. Members of the group groom and scent-mark each other and strangers are chased away. They feed mostly on the ground, always alert, and scatter to the nearest tree when they perceive danger. They have an acute sense of hearing. They often sit in a safe spot from where they mock a predator, jerking their tails.

Voice A bird-like "chook-chook-chook" sound, which grows louder and follows more rapidly till it changes into a rattling sound.

Breeding 1 to 3 young are born any time of the year (peaking in October to April), after a gestation period of ± 8 weeks.

Mass ♂ ± 155 g.
  ♀ ± 150 g.

Food Gum, grasshoppers, moths and spiders. Do not drink water.

Life expectancy
± 10 years.

Enemies Leopard, giant eagle owl.

± 3 cm

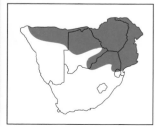

South African Galago

Nagapie
Galago moholi

Description This galago is the smallest of the three galagos. Its fur is much thinner and less woolly (especially the tail) than that of the Greater Galago. Grant's Galago *Galagoides grantii*, a former subspecies of the South African Galago, is browner with yellow underparts, and occurs in parts of Mozambique and Zimbabwe. Its large eyes, bare movable ears and very long hind legs are very characteristic. At night its eyes reflect red in a spotlight.

Sexual dimorphism Males are slightly bigger than females.

Habitat A savannah species which prefers mopane and especially thornveld along streams and rivers.

Habits South African Galagos are gregarious, nocturnal animals, which are active early in the evening and again later at night, just before dawn. They forage on their own at night, but small groups sleep together during the day in a nest high up in a tree or in a hole in a hollow tree trunk. They urinate on their paws and (dominant animals in particular) rub their mammary glands against other galagos in the group. While foraging or on the move, these animals can take immense leaps from tree to tree.

Voice Growl and a "tjak-tjak" sound, which becomes louder.

Breeding 1 to 2 young are born between October and November or from January to February after a gestation period of 4 months.

Also known as Lesser Bushbaby.

Mass ♂ ± 1,22 kg.
♀ ± 1,13 kg.

Food Fruit, gum, insects and also birds and reptiles.

Life expectancy Unknown.

Enemies Leopard, giant eagle owl.

± 4 cm

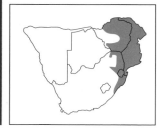

Greater Galago

Bosnagaap
Otolemur crassicaudatus

Description The Greater Galago is the larger of the two galagos. In addition to its bigger size, this galago's fur is much thicker and woollier than that of the South African Galago's, especially its prominent long, thick tall. Its characteristic large eyes and bare movable ears are very prominent. As with the South African Galago, the hind legs are very long and powerful (in comparison with the forelegs), developed for huge jumps between trees.

Sexual dimorphism Males are slightly larger than females.

Habitat Mountain and coastal forest, thickets in woodland with high rainfall and also in riverine forest in drier areas.

Habits These galagos are shy, gregarious animals. They are nocturnal and are sporadically active during the night. They emerge after sunset and first groom themselves before they start feeding. The family group sleeps during the day high up in a tree in thick foliage, but during the night they forage on their own. Greater Galagos have the habit of urinating on their feet and scent-marking one another and their territory with their mammary glands.

Voice An ominous, hoarse wailing.

Breeding 2 young are born from August to September after a gestation period of 4 months.

Also known as Thick-tailed Bushbaby.

Mass ♂ 3,8–8,0 kg. ♀ 3,4–5,2 kg.

Length of tail **Average** ± 65 cm.

Food Mainly wild fruit, flowers, leaves, seeds, insects, birds and eggs.

Life expectancy ± 12 years.

Enemies Leopard, lion, caracal, crowned eagle.

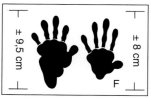

Vervet Monkey

Blouaap
Cercopithecus aethiops

Description A small, light grey monkey with a conspicuously long tail. The belly and flanks are lighter than the upper parts. The face is black and framed with white hair. The feet and the tip of the tail are dark in colour. The male's genitalia are blue. Compared to the Blue Monkey, which also prefers more densely grown forests, the Vervet Monkey is smaller and lighter in colour and does not have black shoulders and legs.

Sexual dimorphism Males are larger than females.

Habitat They prefer woodland, especially on riverbanks, and also favour proximity to human habitat.

Habits These swift tree climbers, which may still be found outside conservation areas, are diurnal and form troops numbering up to 20. Their hierarchy is not as well developed as that of the Baboon. They display aggression towards lower-ranked animals in the troops, by chasing them, or sometimes by merely lifting the eyebrows threateningly. At night they sleep in tall trees and prefer to forage in the early morning. They rest during the heat of day, returning to their sleeping places in the early afternoon.

Voice Chattering and stuttering sounds. The emergency call of the young is a high- pitched scream.

Breeding 1, seldom 2, young are born any time of the year after a gestation period of ± 7 months.

♂

♀

Mass ♂ 8,2–10,0 kg. ♀ 4,5-5,2 kg.

Length of tail **Average** ± 80 cm.

Food Mostly wild fruit, as well as flowers, leaves, sprouts and insects.

Life expectancy Unknown.

Enemy Leopard.

± 9,5 cm   ± 8 cm   F

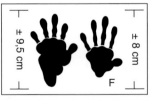

Blue Monkey

Samango-aap
Cercopithecus mitis

Description This rare, little-known monkey has a conspicuously long tail and very tall hind legs. The shoulders, legs and large parts of the tail are black. The face is dark brown and framed with lighter hair. The chest and belly are dull yellow. The rest of the body is light brown, becoming darker with age. It differs from the Vervet Monkey in that it has a heavier build and a darker colour, especially on the legs. It is also more closely associated with forests than the Vervet Monkey.

Sexual dimorphism Males are larger than females.

Habitat Mountain, riverine and coastal forests, and even drier forests.

Habits Blue Monkeys are very shy diurnal animals that spend most of their time in trees. They form troops of 4 to 30 animals, each troop consisting of one or more adult males, the rest being females and young, They sleep at night, and in the heat of the day they rest high up in trees with thick foliage. In the morning they bask in the sun for a while before going out to forage. Foraging is alternated with resting periods. Blue Monkeys are not very aggressive. They generally push their heads forward and raise their eyebrows to muster an aggressive expression designed to keep an inferior in its place.

Voice A high bird-like noise or a "njah" alarm call. Females and young scream and chatter.

Breeding One young is born from September to April after a gestation period of ± 4 months.

Also known as Samango Monkey.

♀

Roger de la Harpe/KZN Parks

♂

Clem Haagner/Gallo

Mass ♂ 27–44 kg.
♀ 4–17 kg.

Length of tail
Average ± 60 cm.

Food Wild fruit, berries, insects, scorpions, meat.

Life expectancy
± 18 years.

Enemies Leopard, lion.

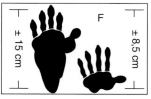

Baboon

Bobbejaan
Papio hamadryas ursinus

Description The Baboon is characterised by its tail: the first part of the tail is carried upwards while the remaining two thirds hang down. The rump displays pinkish callosities. The face is elongated, the eyes are close-set and the nostrils are located at the very end of the snout. The legs are long and the feet are longer than the hands. The colour varies from greyish dull yellow, through shades of brown, to almost black in older males. Newborns are dark in colour with pink faces, ears and feet.

Sexual dimorphism Males are larger and more aggressive than females.

Habitat Very adaptable to any habitat, but prefer mountainous or well-wooded areas.

Habits They form troops of up to 70 individuals, with a distinct hierarchy consisting of a leader supported by one or more dominant males with their family groups. From an early age positions in this hierarchy are constantly contested. At night Baboons sleep on high cliffs or in tall trees, leaving early in the morning to forage and returning to their sleeping places in the late afternoon. The males act as guards while the troops forage. The very young cling to their mothers' bellies, and ride on their mothers' backs when older.

Voice Growl, bark and a warning "bawchom" from the males; screaming and chattering from the young.

Breeding 1, seldom 2, young are born any time of the year after a gestation period of ± 6 months.

Also known as Chacma Baboon.

♂

Burger Cillié

♀

Nigel Dennis/Gallo

SHREWS (family SORICIDAE) are small mouse-like animals with long narrow snouts, small rounded ears, small eyes and musk glands on their flanks. Nocturnal and diurnal.

Naas Rautenbach

Lesser Red Musk Shrew
Crocidura hirta
Klein Rooiskeerbek

The upper parts vary from greyish brown in the east to pale brown in the west, with greyish-white underparts and short tails. Common in suburban gardens where they nest in compost heaps.

Length: ± 15 cm. **Mass:** ± 16 g. **Habitat:** Damp thickets; nest in compost heaps. **Food:** Insects and earthworms. **Breeding:** 1–9 young born Sep-May.

ELEPHANT SHREWS (family MACROSCELIDIDAE) have long moveable snouts, large eyes and ears, and long powerful hind legs. They drum with their hind feet on the ground when alarmed.

Naas Rautenbach

Eastern Rock Elephant Shrew
Elephantulus myurus
Oostelike Klipklaasneus

Greyer than other Elephant Shrews. The flanks are yellow-grey and the belly is white. The patches behind the ears are yellow-brown. Lives in rock crevices. Active at twilight; sun-bathes in the late afternoon.

Length: ± 26 cm. **Mass:** ± 60 g. **Habitat:** Confined to rocky areas. **Food:** Insects; prefers ants and termites. **Breeding:** 1–2 young are born Sep–Apr.

GOLDEN MOLES (family CHRYSOCHLORIDAE) have no visible eyes, ears or tails; the long claws and shovel-like snouts are used for burrowing. Not related to the molerats.

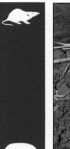

Naas Rautenbach

Hottentot Golden Mole
Amblysomus hottentotus
Hottentot Gouemol

The upper parts are dark reddish brown with a purple to bronze sheen. On the face are tiny white eye-spots. They are subsurface burrowers and do not make hills like molerats.

Length: ± 13 cm. **Mass:** ± 75 g. **Habitat:** Grassland on sandy soils. **Food:** Insects, earthworms, snails and plant material. **Breeding:** 1–2 young born in early summer.

Gambian (Peters')
Epauletted Fruit Bat
Epomophorus gambianus crypturus
Gambiese Witkolvrugtevlermuis

Brownish to nearly white in colour. White patches at the base of the ears; male with white epaulettes on the shoulders. The males' monotonous bell-like call can be heard at night.

Length: 12–15 cm. **Mass:** 80–140 g. **Habitat:** Riverine or other forests with fruit-bearing trees. **Food:** A variety of soft fruit, like wild figs and jackal berry. **Breeding:** 1 (rarely 2) young are born in early summer.

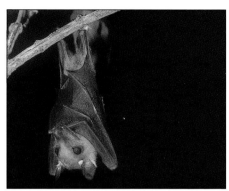

Naas Rautenbach

Wahlberg's Epauletted
Fruit Bat
Epomophorus wahlbergi
Wahlberg se Vrugtevlermuis

Similar to but larger and stouter than the previous species; also with white patches at the base of the ears and white shoulder epaulettes in the male. Colonies roost during the day in the canopy of a tree.

Length: ± 14 cm. **Mass:** 70–110 g. **Habitat:** Riverine and other forests with fruit-bearing trees. **Food:** Soft fruit, like wild figs, moepel and jackal berry. **Breeding:** 1 young born mid-Nov–late Dec.

Naas Rautenbach

Egyptian Rousette
Rousettus aegyptiacus
Egiptiese
Vrugtevlermuis

The upper parts are dark to greyish brown, the underparts are grey. Has a yellowish collar and the throat is brown. Huge colonies rest in caves during the day. Navigates by means of echolocation.

Length: ± 15 cm. **Mass:** 130 g. **Habitat:** Areas with caves and ripe wild fruits. **Food:** Soft fruit. **Breeding:** 1 young born early summer in the north and in late winter in the south.

Naas Rautenbach

207

INSECT-EATING BATS: The tails of Sheath-tailed and Tomb Bats (family EMBALLONURIDAE) are partly enclosed by a membrane. Large eyes and triangular ears well separated on the head.

Burger Cillié

Mauritian Tomb Bat
Taphozous mauritianus
Witlyfvlermuis

The upper parts are grizzled grey and the underparts white, extending onto the wing and tai membrane. They live in pairs, resting fla against vertical tree trunks or rock faces during the day.

Length: ± 11 cm. **Mass:** 28 g. **Habitat:** Oper woodland. **Food:** Insects. **Breeding:** 1 young borr in summer.

FREE-TAILED BATS (family MOLOSSIDAE) have mastiff-like faces. Their tails are partly enclosed by a membrane, with the rest free from the membrane's hind margin.

Naas Rautenbach

Egyptian Free-Tailed Bat
Tadarida aegyptiaca
Egiptiese Losstertvlermuis

They are dark greyish-brown in colour, with a darker head; lacking the lighter neck yoke of the other free-tailed bats. They rest in small colonies in caves, crevices in rocks and hollow trees.

Length: ± 11 cm. **Mass:** ± 15 g. **Habitat:** Range o habitats; usually in more open country. **Food:** Insects caught on the wing. **Breeding:** 1 young born ir summer.

Naas Rautenbach

Little Free-Tailed Bat
Chaerephon pumilus
Klein Losstertvlermuis

Colour varies from blackish brown to brownish grey. The throa is brown and the underparts are yellowish grey. On the neck is a yoke of lighter hair May form large colonies, but usually res close together in small groups in rock crevices or in brickwork.

Length: ± 9 cm. **Mass:** ± 11 g. **Habitat:** Various habitats in open country. **Food:** Insects caught on the wing. **Breeding:** 1 young is born in summe (capable of three cycles per season).

Schreibers' Long-fingered Bat *Miniopterus schreibersii*
Schreibers se Grot-vlermuis

The upper parts are dark brown and the underparts lighter. The wings are almost black. They rest during the day in very large numbers (up to 100 000) in caves. Females have their babies in maternity caves.

Length: ± 11 cm. **Mass:** 10 g. **Habitat:** A range of habitats from arid to well-watered areas. **Food:** Insects. **Breeding:** 1 young born in summer after a gestation period of 8 months.

Naas Rautenbach

Banana Bat
Neoromicia africanus
Piesangvlermuis

The colour varies from dark brown to reddish brown. The underparts are lighter, more greyish brown. It has a large mouth and triangular shaped ears. Small colonies rest during the day inside the curled-up leaf of a banana or strelitzia tree.

Length: ± 8 cm. **Mass:** 4 g. **Habitat:** Moist woodland with banana or strelitzia trees. **Food:** Insects. **Breeding:** 1 young (rarely 2) born early summer.

Naas Rautenbach

Cape Serotine Bat
Neoromicia capensis
Kaapse Dakvlermuis

Dark greyish brown to light greyish brown. The underparts are white to yellowish white and the wings are dark brown. Two or three rest closely together during the day at the base of an aloe leaf or under tree bark. They fly slowly, turning and diving in search of flying insects.

Length: ± 8,5 cm. **Mass:** ± 6 g. **Habitat:** Various habitats, from semi-desert to high rainfall areas. **Food:** Small soft-bodied insects like mosquitoes. **Breeding:** 1–2 young born in summer.

Naas Rautenbach

Slit-faced bats (family NYCTERIDAE) have long ears and a long slit in the middle of the face where the noseleaves are situated. The ultrasonic emissions used in echolocation arise here.

Naas Rautenbach

Egyptian Slit-faced Bat
Nycteris thebaica
Egiptiese Spleetneus-
vlermuis

Colour varies from greyish brown to rufous, with paler underparts. The rest in large colonies in caves and thatched huts. Feed early in the evening and will take spiders and scorpions on the ground.

Length: ± 10 cm. **Mass:** ± 11 g. **Habitat:** A range of habitats. **Food:** Flying insects; also scorpions and spiders. **Breeding:** 1 young born early summer.

Horseshoe bats (family RHINOLOPHIDAE) have complicated noseleaves in the shape of a horseshoe between the mouth and forehead.

Naas Rautenbach

Geoffroy's Horseshoe Bat
Rhinolophus clivosus
Geoffroy se Saalneus-
vlermuis

The upper parts are light brown and the underparts light yellowish grey. Colonies rest during the day in caves and crevices in rocks; hanging from the roof in clusters. They forage alone.

Length: 9,7 cm. **Mass:** 17 g. **Habitat:** Savannahs, also semi-desert. **Food:** Insects. **Breeding:** 1 young born in summer.

Leaf-nosed bats (family HIPPOSIDERIDAE) resemble horseshoe bats, but lack the posterior triangular leaflet. Their ears are large and widely separated.

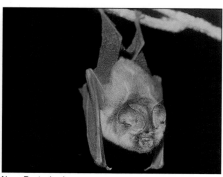

Naas Rautenbach

Sundevall's Roundleaf Bat *Hipposideros caffer*
Sundevall se
Bladneusvlermuis

Colour varies from grey-brown to golden-yellow. The only small bat with this particular formation of noseleaves. They rest during the day in caves, culverts or roofs of buildings.

Length: 9 cm. **Mass:** 8 g. **Habitat:** Savannah woodland. **Food:** Insects. **Breeding:** 1 young born in summer.

Molerats (family BATHYERGIDAE) are endemic to sub-Saharan Africa. They have short legs (the feet adapted to burrowing) and ever-growing, powerful teeth.

African Molerat
Cryptomys hottentotus
Vaalmol • Knaagdiermol

Light grey to dark grey with a white blaze (not always present) on the forehead. Small groups live in burrows marked by mounds of excavated soil.

Length: ± 15 cm. **Mass:** 100–150 g. **Habitat:** Prefers sandy soils; also other soils except clay. **Food:** Bulbs, roots, tubers and underground grass stolons. **Breeding:** Up to 5 young born at any time of the year.

Naas Rautenbach

Dormice (family MYOXIDAE) have squirrel-like tails and soft, dense fur. Have four molar teeth (unlike rats who have only three). Smaller than squirrels; nocturnal.

Woodland Dormouse
Graphiurus murinus
Boswaaierstertmuis

Grey with distinct dark patches around the eyes. The throat and underparts are white. Nocturnal; they live in tree-holes or a nest of grass and leaves.

Length: ± 16 cm. **Mass:** ± 30 g. **Habitat:** Woodland, savannah and even forests. **Food:** Insects, other invertebrates, seeds and other plant matter. **Breeding:** Up to 3 young born in summer.

Naas Rautenbach

Dassie rats (family PETROMURIDAE) are diurnal, squirrel-like animals with a long, hairy (not bushy) tail. They live in rocky areas.

Dassie Rat
Petromus typicus
Dassierot

A squirrel-like "rat" lacking a bushy tail. The colour varies from a speckled grey to dark brown; white to yellowish underparts. Diurnal; lives in family groups. Sunbathes in the morning.

Length: ± 30 cm. **Mass:** ± 200–250 g. **Habitat:** Rocky areas. **Food:** Leaves and flowers, also seeds and fruit. **Breeding:** 2 young born in summer.

Naas Rautenbach

MICE AND RATS: Smaller rodents of the families CRICETIDAE and MURIDAE. The larger species are called rats and the smaller ones mice.

Niel Cillié

Brants' Whistling Rat
Parotomys brantsii
Brants se Fluitrot

Colour is pale yellow brown with whitish under-parts. They are active early in the morning and often sit sunning themselves on a small branch at the entrance of the burrow. Burrows have two or more entrances.

Length: ± 25 cm. **Mass:** ± 120 g. **Habitat:** Dry sandy areas. **Food:** Leaves of succulent plants; also seeds and flowers. **Breeding:** 1–3 young born in summer. Young cling to mother's nipples while she forages.

Naas Rautenbach

Angoni Vleirat
Otomys angoniensis
Angoni Vleirot

Pale to dark brown, with greyish underparts. The very short tail is dark above and paler below, and the ears are very large. Larger than the very similar Vlei Rat. A grass nest is built above water level with runs to its feeding grounds.

Length: ± 30 cm. **Mass:** 100–250 g. **Habitat:** Vleis, swamps and marshy areas along rivers. **Food:** Grass and grass sprouts, also reeds and other plants. **Breeding:** 1–4 young born in summer.

Naas Rautenbach

Single-striped Grass Mouse
Lemniscomys rosalia
Eenstreepmuis

Pale greyish brown in drier areas, to orange brown in higher rainfall areas. The dark stripe down the mid-back is characteristic. Diurnal and usually solitary. Excavates a burrow under matted grass or at the base of a shrub with well-worn runs to its feeding grounds.

Length: ± 27 cm. **Mass:** ± 60 g. **Habitat:** Grassland in bushveld or dry shrubveld. **Food:** Grass and seeds. **Breeding:** 2–5 young born Sep–Mar.

Four-striped Grass Mouse
Rhabdomys pumilio
Streepmuis

Colour varies from pale brick-brown in the west to dark grey-brown in the east. Down the mid-back are four diagnostic stripes. Mainly diurnal; they excavate their burrows under matted grass or at the base of a bush with runs to their feeding grounds. Associated with humans and their surroundings.

Length: ± 19 cm. **Mass:** 30–55 g. **Habitat:** Grassy areas in semi-desert to high-rainfall mountain areas. **Food:** Seeds and other plant material. **Breeding:** 2–9 (usually 5–6) young born in summer.

Niel Cillié

Acacia Rat
Thallomys paedulcus
Boomrot

Yellowish grey, with grey flanks and white under-parts. The black eye-rings form lines that extend to the nose. Nocturnal. They live in trees and nest in tree-holes or sometimes adapt a large bird's nest, lining it with soft plant material. Family groups rest in the nest during the day.

Length: ± 30 cm. **Mass:** ± 100 g. **Habitat:** Savannah woodland, especially *Acacia* woodland. **Food:** Green leaves, fresh seeds, pods; also insects. **Breeding:** 2–5 young born in summer.

Naas Rautenbach

Namaqua Rock Rat
Aethomys namaquensis
Namakwalandse Klipmuis

Reddish- to yellowish brown with white to greyish white underparts. The tail is long. Nocturnal. They live in colonies and nest in rock crevices, tree-holes and at the base of bushes. Huge piles of grass and other plant debris, which they collect for the nest, mark their presence.

Length: ± 26 cm. **Mass:** ± 50 g. **Habitat:** Rocky areas. **Food:** Grass- and other seeds. **Breeding:** 3–5 (up to 7) young born in summer.

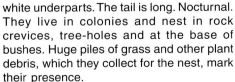

Naas Rautenbach

Naas Rautenbach

Bushveld Gerbil
Tatera leucogaster
Bosveldse Nagmuis

Orange brown to reddish brown; lighter in the west. The tail is dark on top. Nocturnal; they live in loosely associated colonies. One pair usually excavates a burrow with an entrance under a low bush. The burrow is characterised by fresh soil thrown out nightly.

Length: ± 28 cm. **Mass:** ± 70 g. **Habitat:** Sandy soils. **Food:** Grass seeds; other plant matter; insects. **Breeding:** 2–9 young born in summer.

Naas Rautenbach

Pouched Mouse
Saccostomus campestris
Wangsakmuis

The colour is grey in the west and darker greyish brown in the east. The throat and underparts are white. Has a fat body, large head and distinct short tail. Stores food in its cheek pouches to eat later in the safety of the burrow. Nocturnal.

Length: ± 16 cm. **Mass:** ± 45 g. **Habitat:** Various; prefers sandy soils. **Food:** Grass seeds, forbs, shrubs, wild berries; seldom insects. **Breeding:** 2–10 young born in summer.

Naas Rautenbach

Grey Climbing Mouse
Dendromus melanotis
Grysklimmuis

Upper parts are ashy grey (other Climbing Mice are chestnut brown) with a dull dark dorsal stripe and a dark spot on the forehead. Curls its long, semi-prehensile tail around grass stems to steady it while foraging. Builds a small, ball-shaped grass nest just above ground level.

Length: ± 15 cm. **Mass:** ± 8 g. **Habitat:** Tall grass and dense vegetation. **Food:** Grass seeds; insects like moths. **Breeding:** 2–8 young born in summer.

Spoor (Tracks)

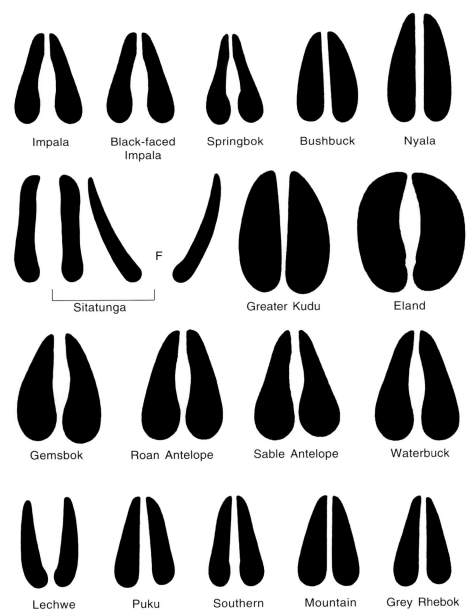

Impala

Black-faced
Impala

Springbok

Bushbuck

Nyala

F

Sitatunga

Greater Kudu

Eland

Gemsbok

Roan Antelope

Sable Antelope

Waterbuck

Lechwe

Puku

Southern
Reedbuck

Mountain
Reedbuck

Grey Rhebok

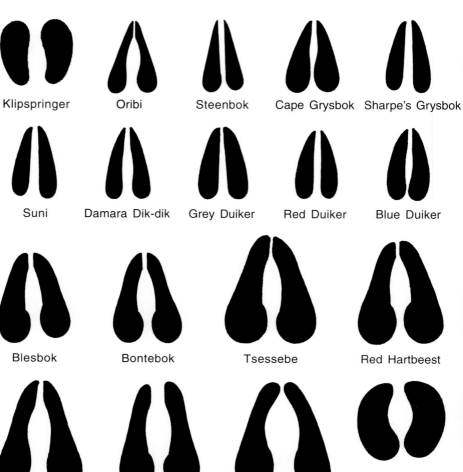

Klipspringer   Oribi   Steenbok   Cape Grysbok   Sharpe's Grysbok

Suni   Damara Dik-dik   Grey Duiker   Red Duiker   Blue Duiker

Blesbok   Bontebok   Tsessebe   Red Hartbeest

Lichtenstein's Hartbeest   Black Wildebeest   Blue Wildebeest   African Buffalo

Plains Zebra   Cape Mountain Zebra   Hartmann's Mountain Zebra

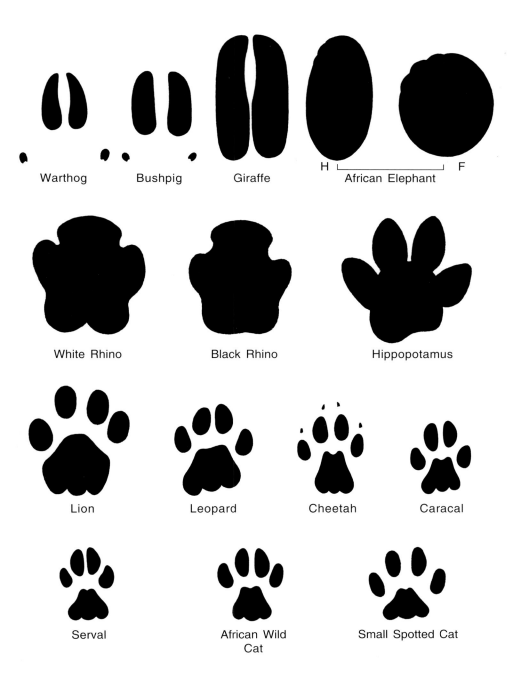

Warthog   Bushpig   Giraffe   African Elephant
H ⊢————————⊣ F

White Rhino   Black Rhino   Hippopotamus

Lion   Leopard   Cheetah   Caracal

Serval   African Wild Cat   Small Spotted Cat

Spotted
Hyaena

Brown
Hyaena

Aardwolf

African Wild
Dog

Side-striped
Jackal

Black-backed
Jackal

Bat-eared
Fox

Cape Fox

Honey
Badger

Civet

Small-spotted
Genet

Large-spotted
Genet

Striped
Polecat

Yellow
Mongoose

Slender
Mongoose

Cape Grey
Mongoose

White-tailed
Mongoose

Marsh
Mongoose

Banded
Mongoose

Dwarf
Mongoose

Meerkat

African
Clawless Otter

Aardvark

Ground
Pangolin

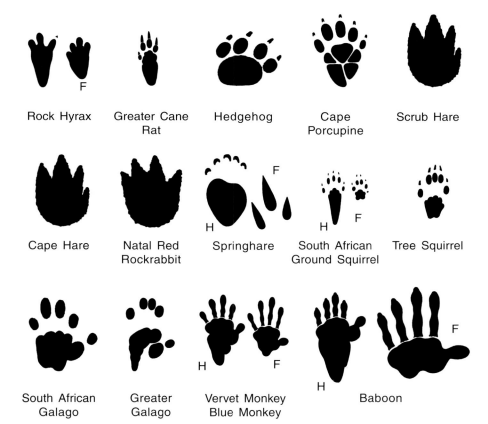

Rock Hyrax

Greater Cane Rat

Hedgehog

Cape Porcupine

Scrub Hare

Cape Hare

Natal Red Rockrabbit

Springhare

South African Ground Squirrel

Tree Squirrel

South African Galago

Greater Galago

Vervet Monkey Blue Monkey

Baboon

References

Bronner, G.N. et al. 2003. A revised systematic checklist of the extant mammals of the southern African subregion. *Durban Mus. Novit.* 28: 56–106.

Brown, L. 1972 *The life on the African plains.* New York: McGraw-Hill.

Cillié, B. 1992. *Sakgids tot Suider-Afrikaanse soogdiere.* Pretoria: J.L. van Schaik Uitgewers.

Clarke, J. & Pitts, J. 1972. *Focus on fauna: the wildlife of South Africa.* Johannesburg: Nelson.

Dorst, J. & Dandelot, P. 1972. *A field guide to the mammals of Africa including Madagascar.* London: Collins.

Liebenberg, L. 1990. *A fieldguide to the animal tracks of Southern Africa.* Cape Town & Johannesburg: David Philip Publishers.

Maberley, C. T.A. 1963. *The game animals of Southern Africa.* Johannesburg: Nelson.

Meester, J.A.J. & Setzer H.W.1971. *The mammals of Africa: an identification manual.* Washington DC: Smithsonian Institute.

National Parks Board of South Africa. 1980. *Mammals of the Kruger and other National Parks.* Pretoria: National Parks Board of South Africa.

Pienaar, U. Dev., Rautenbach, I.L. & De Graaf, G. 1980. *The small mammals of the Kruger National Park.* Pretoria: National Parks Board of South Africa.

Player, I. 1972. *Big game.* Cape Town: Caltex.

Roberts, A. 1952. *The mammals of South Africa.* Johannesburg: CNA.

Roedelberger, F. & Groschoff, V. 1964. *African wildlife.* London: Constable.

Rose, P. 1968. *Big game and other mammals.* Cape Town – Johannesburg: Purnell.

Shortridge, G.C. 1934. *The mammals of South West Africa.* London: Heinemann.

Skinner, J. & Bannister, A. 1985. *Wild animals of South Africa.* Johannesburg: CNA.

Smith, S.J. & Halse A.R.D. 1985. *Rowland Ward' African records of big game.* xxiv Edition, San Antonio, Texas: Rowland Ward Publications, a division of Game Conservation International.

Smithers, R.H.N. 1966. *The mammals of Rhodesia, Zambia and Malawi.* London: Collins.

Smithers, R.H.N. 1983. *The mammals of the southern African subregion.* Pretoria: University of Pretoria.

Stevenson Hamilton, J. *Wildlife in South Africa.* London: Cassel.

Young, E.J., Deeks, J. & Landman, M. 1978. *Beskerm ons seldsame spesies soogdiere van die Transvaal.* Johannesburg: E. Stanton.

Zaloumis, E.A. & Cross, R. *A field guide to the antelope of southern Africa.* Durban: Natal Branch of The Wildlife Society of Southern Africa.

Index